I0476510

Day Trading

Beginners Guide to Building Riches Through the Stock Market

By James Carnegie

James Carnegie

© Copyright 2015 - All rights reserved.

In no way is it legal to reproduce, duplicate, or transmit any part of this document in either electronic means or in printed format. Recording of this publication is strictly prohibited and any storage of this document is not allowed unless with written permission from the publisher. All rights reserved.

The information provided herein is stated to be truthful and consistent, in that any liability, in terms of inattention or otherwise, by any usage or abuse of any policies, processes, or directions contained within, is the solitary and utter responsibility of the recipient reader. Under no circumstances will any legal responsibility or blame be held against the publisher for any reparation, damages, or monetary loss due to the information herein, either directly or indirectly.

Respective authors own all copyrights not held by the publisher.

Legal Notice:

This book is copyright protected. This is only for personal use. You cannot amend, distribute, sell, use, quote or paraphrase any part or the content within this book without the consent of the author or copyright owner. Legal action will be pursued if this is breached.

Disclaimer Notice:

Please note the information contained within this document is for educational and entertainment purposes only. Every attempt has been made to provide accurate, up to date and reliable complete information. No warranties of any kind are expressed or implied. Readers acknowledge that the author is not engaging in the rendering of legal, financial, medical or professional advice.

By reading this document, the reader agrees that under no circumstances are we responsible for any losses, direct or indirect, which are incurred as a result of the use of information contained within this document, including, but not limited to, —errors, omissions or inaccuracies.

Table of Contents

Introduction

Are you looking to improve your finances? Planning to manage your investments better and create wealth, but intimidated by the stock market and other popular investment options? An opportunity called "day trading" or "options trading" is the solution you need. If you are willing to take minimal risk in the process of making some good money, "*options*" trading is a fantastic opportunity. An opportunity, if rightly used whilst carefully treading the pitfalls that it comes bundled with, can put you on the path to making a lot of money, enough in some cases, to fund your own yacht or mansion, of course with due respect to the risks involved.

This book will introduce you to the basics of option trading – what it is, and why one should be interested in it, basic jargon like the types of options, how to trade options, strategies, do's and don'ts and a useful cheat sheet that will assist you in making the right choices while investing.

People in general tend to invest in the stock market without much research or information about the intricacies of trading stock. These uninformed decisions tend to result in poor yields, in turn leading to demotivation. After a few initial unsuccessful ill-informed attempts, one quits, thinking that it's all hype surrounding making money with stock trading.

For someone who has always wanted to enter the world of trading but hasn't had the money or right information to start with stock trading, starting off with trading "options" as a first step. But become comfortable first and have a better idea about trading before plunging into stock trading.

There is always a lot of information floating around – mostly talking about the money that one can make, without giving due information about the risks involved with trading. It is always best advised therefore to become familiar with the theory and gain some knowledge before experimenting with investing in the market.

This book plans to bridge that gap and demystify the world of investment and throw some light on trading – "options" in particular, such that it'll not only get you interested in trading but also get you acquainted with the necessary data for getting into the big league.

James Carnegie

Chapter 1
Why Is Day Trading the Perfect Way to Get Wealthy?

In my opinion, day trading is the perfect way to make vast profits, and here are the reasons why:

Day trading is the ultimate 'equal opportunity' investment

When it comes to day trading, it doesn't matter whether you have a PhD or you are a college dropout, male or female, young and inexperienced or old and seasoned; you could be trading from a jail in Mexico or from a mansion in Beverly Hills. As long as you have sufficient funds, you will have similar chances of success or failure to everyone else trading on the same platform. This is a result of everybody ultimately trading in the same place, which is the stock market. So if all of you belong to the same country and choose the same markets and pick the same stocks, then how can each one of you have different results? It really does not take a genius to pick the stocks, as you only have to make use of a little intelligence and choose the ones that will surely give you results. So choosing to day trade will make your life easier and help you double or even triple your existing money.

No need to hire employees

Due to the fact that you will be executing trades yourself, you will not need to conduct interviews, implement payroll or conduct employee evaluations. As a day trader, your only team member will be your broker. You never have to worry about your broker because when you are dissatisfied with one, there are always ten others ready to take up his place. Also, there will come a time when you will do away with your broker as well. Once you understand how everything happens, you will garner the confidence to execute the trades yourself. You will buy and sell the stocks in the market using the software provided to you and all you have to do is login and conduct the trade. Imagine the amount of money and time that can be saved. You will get accustomed to setting your daily stock work time as just 5 hours a day and not more.

You just need a phone and a computer to trade

Unlike most forms of investment today, with day trading you will never need to have a "bricks and mortar" office, tedious inventory files or any other equipment besides your computer and phone. This means you will not be tied down in one place or have to worry about insurance, marketing, or hefty rent . You can work from wherever you can access the Internet. You can even do away with your bulky computer and use just a tablet. That will be sufficient for you to login to your software and buy and sell your stocks.

Trading requires minimal time

Another great benefit of venturing into day trading is that it demands very little of your time. This is why many people venture into day trading and continue to hold on to their 9 to 5 jobs that demand 40 hours of their lives every week. You can decide to trade full-time or part-time, the whole day or as little as an hour a day and still realize healthy profits from your trades. All you have to do is get acquainted with the ways of day trading and understand how these stocks are traded on a daily basis. You will not hold onto the financial assets of any company overnight, instead buying and selling these stocks within a single day. So that means no waiting overnight to see the performance of your stocks. This quick result is what makes day trading such a lucrative option for all those looking to take it up as a full time job.

Low capital requirement

To get started in day trading, you do not need to be filthy rich, or take a large loan to see realistic returns. We will talk about how realistic it is to get started with, but to give you an idea on how flexible this form of investment is, starting capital of $1,000 is enough to generate decent profits for a beginner. In fact, if you are thinking of day trading seriously then you can pick a class of stock known as penny stocks. These stocks will be extremely low price (hence, "penny stocks") so you won't have to spend a lot. You can capitalize on the difference in their prices and reap the profit. Thus with a minimalinvestment, you can successfully buy the stocks of a company and also sell them to come into a substantial profit.

Instantaneous returns

When you talk of day trading, you talk of 'fast cash'. This form of trading converts trades into profit within seconds. Where else could you invest and see your money multiply within minutes? You can buy and sell at the click of a button and see your profits grow from those trades. In most other forms of investments e.g. real estate or online businesses, it takes weeks, months or even years for investors to realize returns on their investments. All it takes is for you to pick the stocks that will move from their low to their high within a single day. In fact, it takes no more than a few minutes for this to happen and you will see your results in no time. It is best that you take up day trading, as opposed to long term trading, as the former will give you better results as compared to the latter and improve your chances of increasing your monthly gains. After all, who would say no to their money doubling or tripling within a single day?

Easy to learn to trade

Finally, to be a master in day trading, you would not need to attend a four-year college course or pay an instructor to lecture you every evening. Unlike many other investment types that require you to be a professional with years of training and experience, day trading can be learned in days and a wise investor can become a successful trader in no time.

To get started as a day trader, you will need:

- A computer with a decent internet connection

- Charting software

- A broker

- An adequately funded trading account

- A sound trading strategy

These essential requirements are discussed in more detail in chapter 7: Getting started in day trading.

Chapter 2
About Options

There are numerous avenues available to the investor to manage their wealth and make investments such as mutual funds, bonds, and stocks. However, the opportunities to invest don't end with such traditional investment options, as there is another powerful way to trade that is called "day trading" or "trading options" – a very versatile method of making some money through trading.

"Day trading" is a great opportunity to make quick, safe money by trading stocks within a day's exchange – hence the name. The reason why "options" are considered an extremely powerful opportunity is because of their flexibility, allowing the user to make amends at any time throughout the trading phase. The trader can choose to play both extremely safe and conservative or take the plunge and go to the speculative end of the trading spectrum where the risk of losing is as high as the option of making a large profit! It is no secret that no investment is safe from losses but there are some that might pay more and pose only a slight risk. Not to say that "options" will help you make high profits alone but might not carry as much risk as investing in mutual funds and bonds.

So what are these "options" and how are they different from traditional stock trading?

Let me first give a quick simple comparison; assume there are a bunch of traders, and stocks of company A are available in the market. The average price of good company stocks are quite high – let assume say they are $200 for representational purposes.

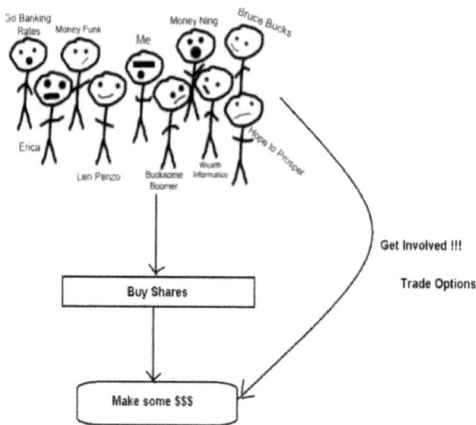

Ideally how one makes money is by buying a share of such stocks of a given company, say 10 stocks of $200 each, which is a lot of money that not everyone has to invest. The person will have to raise $2,000, which is not always easy to do, even if many can afford it. However, those that can afford it fall into the minority. The rest might as well consider "options".

After investing in the stocks of the company, one sells a portion and all of the shares back in the market when the prices are suitable to either make a profit or to avoid complete loss. However, like any trade, no one can ever be sure of how the market sways, thus making the option of trading stocks a very risky one. Now say the person gets to sell the shares for $210 each, then the profit will come up to $100. But most people don't sell at such a small profit and wait until the profit margin rises to at least double the stock's price. However, that could take 4 to 5 years or more, depending on the market conditions and how well the company is faring. It is not everybody's cup of tea to wait out that kind of time and there will be many who will remain restless. For these people "options" represent a good choice.

On the other hand, "options" allow the traders to skip the intermediate step of buying stocks and go directly to the making money part, allowing investors to get directly involved with trading without actually buying stocks! That's right, the person has a chance to deal in stocks without having to buy them, wait for them to grow in value and then sell them. It is possible to jump to the final step of trading in the market.

An "option" is therefore a solution to problems that many new traders face in the world of stocks. Not all new entrants will have the confidence to invest in stocks and will look for a safe place to start with. "Options" allow you to do a lot more than traditional stock, allowing one to gamble on a changing stock index from a shielded position, thus cushioning yourself in case there is a market crash. So it is a safe bet to invest in stocks and avoid market risks.

However, as cozy as it sounds, "options" that are used in day trading also come with their own limitations and risks, which if not handled properly, could leave one with heavy losses. As was said before, no investment is free from risks and "options" also come with their fair share. It would be foolish to think that just by opting for "options", it will be possible to make a huge profit and turn rich within a month. If it worked that way, then every other person would be a millionaire. It is far from impossible to convert your hundred dollar bills into thousands but it will require you to pay keen attention to your trading.

"Options" are multifaceted, uncertain, contain risks and are definitely not for everyone, which is a reason why someone might advise you to keep away from the world of day trading. Well, but what is life without a little well-informed, calculated risk? No risk no gain - it's vital to take a little risk from time to time. You never know, you might make it big and live to speak about it! Whether you take the plunge to trade or not, isn't it better to know a little bit about an investment option, instead of deceived into trading "options" without knowledge? You will have a better insight into the things that you need to do while trading "options".

By the end of this book, you'll have a basic idea of trading. You can even read further and start practicing in order to learn the tricks of the trade. Remember, all those traders out there did not start out successful, -it'staken them years of experience to be where they are. You might think of it as being slightly daunting but if you use the right techniques, you will have a chance to make it big in the world of stock trading.

An "option" is basically an agreement, which provides the buyer a legal entitlement (but not an obligation) to buy/sell at a precise value for a given stock on or before a specific date. It is like insurance for a stock or a bond; however, the agreement is well defined with clear conditions and terms.

 It might still be ambiguous, so let's take a real life example to understand what an "option" is. For example, you find a car that was likely to have been used in a Bond movie, but the authenticity is not verified yet. You would like to buy it, however you do not have the necessary finance to buy the vehicle for another few weeks – say 2 weeks.

You make an agreement with the car dealer such that you have a possibility of buying the car in 2 weeks for $x. The dealer agrees to it, but in return to this deal offered, you pay an advance fee of $y.

At this point, two things could happen:

1.   The car was indeed the original car that was used in the movie, and this means the car price rises steeply to a

few thousand dollars more than the originally agreed $x price. But because you already made a deal with the car dealer, he has to now sell the car to you for $x, which means you can sell the car for the new higher price value and take the extra money for profit.

2.   However, on the contrary, if you find the car is actually not in a good condition needinga lot of repair and making it is almost valueless. At this point, you can take a decision to not buy the car, thus saving $x, however you will lose $y which you made as an initial payment.

Now the deal in that example can be mapped to "options", and the car to the actual stock and so forth, and that gives a clear picture of the exact benefits of trading options. First, it gives you the choice: you can always go back on a deal if you see that it's going toturn out lousy. "Options" are also called "derivatives" for this very reason, that is, an "option" derives its worth by relying on something else. Here, the result can be anything and you will have to trust your instinct. More than instinct, it is important to trust your judgment in understanding whether the stock will work out to be a good "bet". This can be hard to do in the beginning but can get easier as you go.

Let us look at a monetary example for you to understand it better.

Suppose A offers you 100 shares of company XYZ for $50 each. So he is expecting you to pay him $5,000 for them. But you tell him you will pay him $1000 in advance and pay the rest later, in say 2 weeks' time. He agrees and keeps the shares for you. During the two-weeks, you find out that the company is superb and that its share prices are going to rise due to favorable news breaking out. In the week that you are meant to pay him, the price per share has risen to $60. Now, you will still have to pay him the difference of the amount after deducting the $1m000 that you had already paid him. This is because he had agreed to give you the shares at $50 each, which means you got it at a great discount. You can then sell it at $60 and makea profit for it. However, in case the price drops to $40 due to, let's say, bad news about the company doing the rounds, the seller will still demand $50 for the shares. But if you think it is not worth your money then you can refuse to pay it. Here, you will have to part with your $1,000 that you had paid as an advance but will have the chance to save $4,000 in the process. That refusal to pay is your "option". In all this, your seller will always wish for the price to drop whereas you as a buyer will wish for the price to rise. In most cases, the price always rises, as there is a constant demand for shares in the market. But you never know when the prices might change direction as nothing is guaranteed in the stock market so it could go either way.

It is understandable that you will have a lot of doubts in treading this path in the beginning and might need a lot of help in trusting this line of investment. But as was mentioned earlier, it will get easier for you once you get the hang of it and you will be in a position to make the right choices for yourself. In this next segment, we will look at why trading with "options" is a good choice for beginners.

Why Trade with Options?

Though we understand that "options" give the investor the advantage of getting involved with trading without actually having to buy stocks, there are a few more compelling points as to why one should consider trading with "options".

1.   The scope to speculate is the biggest strength of trading with "options". As was cited in the example above,

it is possible for you to speculate as to what the stocks can be worth. If you use your wits and are capable of speculating correctly, you will have a chance to hit the jackpot, all within the same day. Speculation is nothing but legitimate betting, which will enable you to either gain money, if done wisely, or lose out. Remember, when trading with "options," one should be able to speculate and predict the direction in which the stocks go and strike a deal on stocks which are likely to have a better price rise. A combination of how the price changes within a specific time period plus the commissions involved, plays a great factor in making effective use of speculation for making good money with "options" trading. You will always enjoy speculating and the more you do it, the more you start to predict correctly. Now, don't compare this with "normal" gambling as there, you will have only a few choices to pick from, like picking between teams A and B. Here, the "options" market puts forth an ample number of choices for you to pick from and depending on your choice and needs, you can pick the best stocks and trade with them.

2.   The second good reason is called "hedging". Hedging is nothing but an insurance, which is what "options" are to

your stocks as they insure you against potential losses that might incur if a stock fails. Though purists in the stock market trading scene may argue that it is unwise to make an investment on stocks that you think will not reap you profits, there could always be cases where you want to take a risk – for example, with new technology stocks- which could reap huge profits. Attention though is needed, as you cannot always be too sure about them. So instead of not investing at all, "options" are a great way to take careful risks and cushion against any potential failure by using effective hedging strategies. As we saw in the example, a person can make a profit of $1,000 on the investment but will get to save $4,000 on it. So it is a wiser choice for you to adopt such a strategy as opposed to "gambling" away your $5,000.

3.   A third reason is that, trading in options presents the opportunity for you to take advantage of the market's unlimited profit potential while enjoying limited risks. This is one of the biggest advantages "option" trading has compared to outright stock trading. The reason for this is that "option" buyers have a right, not an obligation, to exercise the contract for the set price. When the price is not

favorable at the time of expiration, a buyer can choose to forfeit the right and just let the contract expire without actually buying the underlying stock. Other investments in the market do not offer you this opportunity. It is like saying you wish to buy a house, reserve it and then decide not to buy it at the last minute. Whether you like it or not, you will have to buy it and pay in full for it. This does not apply to the "options" market where you can decide to walk away from a deal if you don't think it is a lucrative option for you.

4.   You already know that the buyer of an "options" contract puts down a payment known as premium to the "options" writer or the seller. The amount that the buyer pays is basically the amount paid for the "option" although there is more about the price. When you pay the premium to an "option" seller, you are not actually buying anything and no asset will be transferred to you until you decide to exercise the purchase. This is basically an agreement that lets the buyer choose if and when the transfer of the "option" will take place. However, the underlying asset – the stock, determines the value of the "options" contract. The amount of shares the buyer gets is the number of

"option" contracts multiplied by the contract multiplier (also called the contract size). Because small investors can get to take advantage of leveraging – trading very large exposure while outlaying only a small amount of capital, this form of investment is very attractive.

Apart from these obvious reasons for trading "options", another interesting characteristic is that a lot of the stock "options" of huge corporations are not available to the public, as they are offered exclusively to the companies' employees via a program called ESP – Employee Stock Exchange as part of their benefits package. This aspect of exclusivity is a great deal for both; for the companies, in that they get to retain the best talent but also for the employees, who areat an advantage when the company's stocks are doing great.

The employees will work hard towards helping the company making it big. It is possible for an employee to hold on to the stocks even if he or she quits. Several employees who had invested in companies such as Apple and Microsoft had the chance to sell their stocks once the companies made it big and they became millionaires overnight. Similarly, if your company is offering a chance to buy stocks then you must make use of the opportunity. However, it is important to check whether the stock is doing well in the market. If it is, then you can buy and hold it for a long time. Once the price of the stock reaches its lifetime high, you can decide to sell it in the market and profit from it.

These are just some of the advantages of "options" but it is not limited to these. You will understand what the others are once you actually start trading in them on a daily basis.

Chapter 3

Basic Types of Options

Now that we've got a basic idea about what "options" are and have illustrated reasons good enough for you to be interested in the idea of trading "options", let's get down to understanding a little more theory. For example, the types of "options" available and the different players in the day trading market. You can read through them thoroughly in order to understand the best option for you.

Binary Options can be of two basic types:

1.   Call Option

2.   Put Option

A 'call' option basically allows you to buy at a given price for a given period of time. Buyers of call options are basically optimistic that the stock prices will go up and can make better profit before the stocks drop.

Some key parameters that define an "option" to be "call option" are:

- The underlying stock or index

- The option has an expiry date

- The strike price of the option

- The option gives the "right to BUY" a stock / index.

To understand call and put options better, it is important to understand a few basic jargon terms and the basic process involved.

Let's take the example of stock A which is priced at $10, and you as a trader expect the stock to at least go up by $1 and end at $11 – which is called the "strike price", before closing the deal for the stock, in say a couple of weeks.

Because you expect the price to go up by $1, the actual price that you'll be paying to make the trade is $1.00; this is the price of your deal/ "option".

This means, if the stock price reaches $11, you will break even and make a profit, even if the stock goes up a few cents beyond $11 in those couple of weeks. Otherwise you might be at a loss, and in this case you will lose $1 per call option.

The value of a call option is therefore the difference between the strike price ($11) that you predicted and the actual price that the stock rose or fell to.

If we assume that the stock price went up to $20 at the end of 2 weeks, the value of call option is $9 and that's also the profit that you make per call option.

But, if the stock price drops to $8 at the end of 2 weeks, which is the specified time, then it will result in a loss. However, it is not possible for you to know whether there will be an increase or a decrease based on speculation. Most people don't bother with small losses especially in the beginning as it helps them learn the market better. The next time that they decide to invest, they are much more cautious and know where to and where not to invest their money.

The following graphs will help visualize the call options and the profit that can be made with them better. Call options are also called "Long Term" options because of the possibility of unlimited "maximum profit" that they can offer.

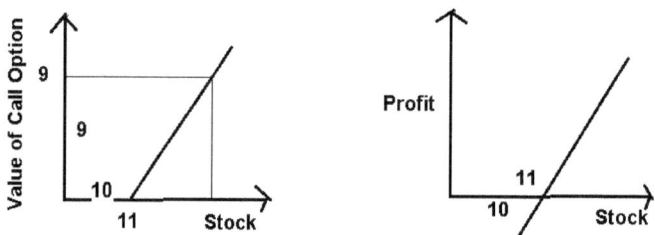

So, from the graphs it can be seen how the price of stocks increasing or decreasing determines the profit that you can make with the "options" and the strike rate that you can fix.

2. The second type of "option" is called the 'put' options or "exotic" options. It provides the buyer the chance to sell a financial resource at a strike price before a definite expiry time. Put options are similar to having the power to take a short decision on stocks while trading. Like the name suggests, it literally allows you to make money by selling the stock at a predicted strike price. Here, the profit is made when the stocks lose money; this is therefore a riskier but interesting trade method, which is better used after

much experience is gained in the field. Buyers of put options basically believe and hope that the price of a stock, whose options they hold, will in reality reduce by an x amount, x, before the close of business so that they can make some money.

Let us assume that stock B is currently priced at $10, and you then speculate and predict based on a number of parameters that the price is most likely to fall by $1, so you pay a price of $2 to buy the stock that will expire in 2 weeks. In this period, the profit that one makes is limited by the following formula,

Max Profit = $11 - $2

= $9

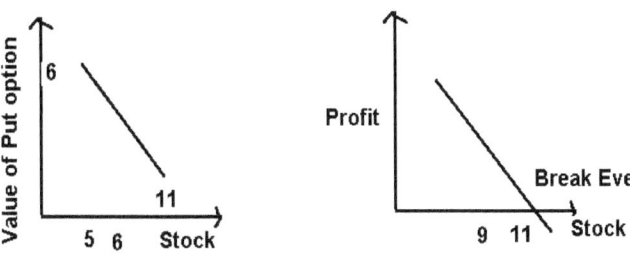

This stock option basically limits the profit that one can make.

In both these cases, it is ideal to try and break even if it is not possible to make a profit. This will ensure that you are not undergoing a loss and will make back the money that you put in. It will also prevent you from feeling bad about having chosen the wrong type of "option". Although there is no particular favorite, some people prefer the put option as there is no such timeframe and it is easier for him or her to trade. But, there are also those who will like the call option as well so it is entirely up to you.

The above dealt with the types of stock options available in the market for trading; now it is time to understand the various players in the day trading market.

There are four key players whose role one must understand before starting with day trading. These are:

1.   Buyers of calls

2.   Vendors of calls

3.   Buyers of puts

4.   Vendors of puts

Another piece of jargon that one should be familiar with, is the name for how individuals who buy and trade "options". They are referred to as "holders", and those individuals who sell "options" are called "writers". Also, those buyers are said to have long positions and the sellers short positions respectively.

Here are some key points to remember about what these individual players can and cannot do in the trading market:

1.   It is not compulsory for "holders" – that is the buyers of call and put "options", to buy or sell the stocks as such. They have complete freedom to choose to do so at their own discretion if they wish to do so.

2.   Writers or sellers of call and put options are however obliged to buy/sell the stocks. This means it's important for them to better assess how they trade.

Since it can be understood that selling "options" is a high-risk process as it is a little more complicated and requires more practice and experience, this book will focus primarily on trading from the perspective of the "buyer" alone. For now, just knowing that there are players in the market who can sell "options" is sufficient to start off with.

James Carnegie

Chapter 4
More Jargon!

For any business or job, it is important for one to get familiarized with the buzzwords or jargon in order to be able to communicate effectively and to better understand what is going on. This section will focus on introducing you to some elementary vocabulary required with respect to day trading.

1. You will probably already be familiar with the very basic and rudimentary terms of trading such as "**stock**", "**calls**" and "**puts**". In any case, here is a brief description of the three. Stocks are the shares of a company. They are a part of the company that is issued to the public in order for them to have a stake in the ownership of the company. Calls and puts were explained in detail in the previous segment. However, as a brief summary, calls refer to the

right of a person to buy a stock from a trader by setting a set price for it. Once the stock reaches the right price, the customer will pay for it in full and buy the stock. The put option gives the trader the right to sell the stocks to a customer.

2. **Strike Price**: This is another term that was introduced in the previous chapter when discussing call and put options. This term refers to the value at which the players in the market can trade a given financial component. This is the value that the price of a stock should either exceed (for calls) or go below (for puts) in order to make profits. 3. **Expiry Date**: This is another important aspect of day trading that one should remember, because all trading (selling /buying) of a particular option needs to be done before the expiry date of a given "option". Otherwise the deal gets terminated and essentially becomes valueless. You might have to pay attention to this small detail when you decide to trade in "options". You might have to deal with a loss if you surpass the expiry date. You can have reminders to help you remember or have someone who is helping you remind you. There is no set time for these "options" but most people prefer to keep it short, as waiting

too long on it might leave it vulnerable to fluctuations in the market, which can negatively affect the financial security's price. 4. A concept needed to comprehend in order to understand the money involved, is what we call the "**intrinsic value**" – it is simply the sum of how the "option" is "in-the-money" for a given option. In the case of calls, it is said to be "in-the-money" if the share price is above the strike price and vice versa in the case of puts.

5. Options that are traded over the National Options exchange, like the CBOE (Chicago Board Options Exchange), are called registered "options" and are the safest and reliable to trade. These "options" which are classified as, "**registered options,**" should have a definitive strike price and expiration date. Any such "option" is equivalent to 100 shares of the enterprise level stock as identified in the contract.

6. **Premium**: The total price of an "option" is referred to as the "premium." This price is determined by calculating aspects such as the time remaining before the expiration, the stock price itself, the strike price, the amount of volatility of a given stock and the time value. This aspect of trading – calculating the premium -is therefore a complex

one which is beyond the scope of a beginner, and better attempted after some experience.

7._**Covered Calls**: When the seller of the call option chooses to retain the indebted value of the stock, this short call is called a "covered call". This provides the stockowner with some additional profit by means of allowing intermittent selling of the call options.

8. **Uncovered or Naked Calls**: If a call is written without mandating a hold of underlying security, it is referred to as shorted uncovered. This kind of uncovered selling is highly risky and definitely not a recommended option for a newbie as it is extremely dangerous and volatile.

9. **Call Spreads**: A call spread is a policy by way of which an equivalent amount of a call option's arguments are bought and sold immediately on the same stock but at different strike prices and / or expiry dates. This scheme minimizes the trader's chances at a make or break loss scenario. However, this doesn't come for free, as it comes at the cost of limiting one's prospective profit on trading the given call option.

Similarly, there are covered and uncovered "options" and spreading scheme for puts options as well.

10. **Buying to open**: when you want to buy a call or put option, you are buying to open a situation, you will be either "buying calls to open" or "buying puts to open."

11. **Selling to Close**: Let us take an example that you want to buy a call option for $5, and through the next couple of weeks, the price of the "options" you bought, went up to $7. Now if you choose to sell to close the trade, this is called selling to close. Basically you bought something and started a trade, now you sold something to close what you started.

12. **Selling to Open**: Remember in case of put options, the way one trades and makes profit is actually by "selling", which means one will start trading by "selling an option". Let us take the case that you are an "optionswriter" and you intend to sell a "covered call"; the expression which refers to this is called "selling a call option to open". This basically puts one in a position to earn a good income by selling.

13. **Buying to Close**: This is similar to the previous case but vice versa. Where one buys "options" to close out a "covered call "state, one needs to close the deal by buying

the option that one pledged to sell. This case is therefore known as "buying to close" an order case.

Types of options

Remember that there are two types of "options" that you can choose from, one being European options and the other American options.

American options

American "options" are those that you can buy in full and dispose of at any point in time, regardless of whether the expiry date is near or far. This is a good option as you can capitalize on the stock's current position. Say for example that you buy a stock today. You can trade in full within a few days and not have to wait for a year or so. This is the most traded form of "options" in the world and it is best that you choose this type.

European options

European "options" are those that you cannot sell until a specified period of time. Even if the stock is doing well now, you will have to hold on to it in vain. This type is not common and also not preferred, as you will probably end up undergoing losses by choosing it.

Note that these are only names given to the "options" and they have absolutely no geographical relevance whatsoever.

James Carnegie

Chapter 5
How to Read Options Tables and How to Trade Options

Let us see a quick example to understand how to trade "options". Assume a company ABC, whose stock price is at $27 on April 1st with a premium of $2.17 for a June 30 call. This simply means the expected strike price is $30 for the month of June.

The total price of the "option's" trade contract will be the premium * 100 shares, which in our case is equal to $2.17 * 100 = $217. Therefore, to make any profit, the price should rise above the fixed strike rate and also keeping in mind the premium, the point of breakeven will be $29.17.

So, at this point, as long as the stock price remains at $27, you are not going to make any money, in fact you are in debt for the $217 that you had to pay to hold the contract.

Now assume that after 4 weeks, the stock prices shoot up to $37. Now the difference in stock price is $10, however since the premium was $2.17, this has to subtracted from $5, which gives us $7.83, which leaves us the whooping value of $7.83 * 100 = $783!!

At this point, you can choose to sell the "option" to close and make a profit that is almost double, or you can continue to hold the "options" speculating that the stock prices could go up even further. Remember you still have time before the contract expires.

However, if the stock prices drop to either $32 or even $26, you are bound to hit losses, as not only does the contract become valueless and you not making profit but you also lose the premium you paid to buy the "options" contract.

Therefore, it is important to speculate wisely and close the deals at the most appropriate time possible. This price swing is the leverage in action handling, which basically determines the success of day trading.

One other important aspect that needs to be understood at this juncture is the concept of intrinsic value and time value.

The fluctuations in our premium value over a period of time can be best explained using the concept of intrinsic value and time value.

Premium of option = Time Value + Intrinsic Value

Intrinsic value is basically the amount of money, which is the price of the stock that equals the strike price. The time value component mentioned in the formula above basically denotes the possibility of the value of the option increasing over a period of time between the points of making the contract to the expiration period.

So that is the basic idea of how "options" are traded; however, in reality, one does not always exercise the right to buy / sell the underlying stock. Instead, the holders tend to make profit by closing out their position by selling to the market, where the writers buy the "options". An interesting piece of trivia with respect to "options" traded in the market is shared by the National Exchange, stating that only 10% of actual trading happens by exercising the right to buy / sell, the majority is by means of trade-off only.

With more and more people becoming familiar with "option" trading, either to speculate the direction of stocks or using "options" as a hedge, there is plenty of information available in the market. Therefore, it is imperative to learn how to interpret the data available in the "options" table, which is published by the stock exchanges, or company's financial reports which are published online. The general format of the "options" table that is seen most often looks like this:

Source: Internet

View By Expiration: **May 2015** | Jun 2015 | Jul 2015 | Oct 2015 | Jan 2016 | Jan 2017

Call Options		Expire at close Friday 22 May 2015					
Strike	Symbol	Last	Chg	Bid	Ask	Vol	Open Int

130.00	IBM150515C00130000	**39.19**	0.00	40.75	44.50	22	16
150.00	IBM150515C00150000	**20.30**	0.00	21.00	24.00	1	6
155.00	IBM150515C00155000	**18.30**	0.00	16.15	18.60	800	21
157.50	IBM150515C00157500	**13.70**	0.00	13.65	16.25	9	9
160.00	IBM150515C00160000	**12.75**	⬆ **1.18**	12.25	12.90	5	194
160.00	IBM150529C00160000	**13.09**	0.00	11.70	14.25	50	25
162.50	IBM150515C00162500	**7.90**	0.00	9.65	10.40	5	25
162.	IBM150529C0	**10.**	0.00	9.4	11.	10	20

50	0162500	**49**	0	0	65	0	
165.00	IBM150515C00165000	**7.75**	↑ **1.00**	7.65	7.95	45	500
165.00	IBM150522C00165000	**5.66**	0.00	7.60	8.90	22	23
165.00	IBM150529C00165000	**7.89**	0.00	7.85	9.30	1	2
167.50	IBM150515C00167500	**5.25**	↑ **1.05**	5.25	5.60	5	180
167.50	IBM150522C00167500	**5.25**	0.00	5.60	6.70	3	43
167.50	IBM150529C00167500	**4.50**	0.00	6.05	7.00	1	167

The second column shows the underlying stocks, whereas the bid and ask column are important to note (for understanding). How these are calculated are however beyond the scope of this book.

Some Useful Strategies and Common Rules On Trading

A lot has been discussed about "options" and how to work with them, but here are some simple rules of thumb strategies, that one can employ to make a judgement on trading "options" and actually making some profit.

Rule 1: If the market is looking positive – going up, buy call options / sell put options. Similarly, if the market is going down, do the opposite – sell calls, buy puts. Selling is always a better strategy than buying. You will have a chance to make quite a profit. However, you must understand which ones will bring in the best value when sold. Seek the help of a friend who deals in stocks and ask for sound advice. Once you understand how it is done, you will be able to sell with confidence. As soon as you realize that the market is looking up, you can decide to sell your stocks. Do it fast and don't think it will go higher than where it already is. Treading carefully in the "options" market should be your number 1 rule to follow and one you should stick with it even if you turn into a pro.

Rule 2: Always let the first hour of the day pass by, and notice if the market of the stock you are interested in is going in the same direction as it was in the morning or increasing, and if it is, make an "at-the-market" buy. Many new traders decide to buy within the first few seconds of the market opening and end up taking heavy losses. You have to tread carefully and intelligently in the stock market if you wish to make positive progress. Doing things in haste will only cause you to lose money and will most likely end up having heavy losses at the end of the trading day!

Rule 3: Always remember to observe the trend and to speculate wisley ! Even if it takes you a month or two to understand the stock, spend at least 2 hours a day just observing how the stock is moving. If you are able to establish a set pattern, then it is best that you start trading in those stocks and predict them to remain in profits.

Rule 4: Do notever buy something simply because it's cheap! This temptation to buy something unwanted simply because it's available at a cheaper price is a big pitfall one must avoid – this is popularly dubbed as "The Price Tag problem". For all you know, the company that you are buying from is horrible and is consistently declaring losses. You will end up buying from such a company and undergo major losses. If it is cheap today, then understand that it may be cheap forever. There are success stories of certain stocks starting small and going big no doubt, but that will not always happen and you might be stuck with a slow movingstock for a very long time. So tread carefully and avoid such unwanted stocks.

Rule 5: Do not commit more than 5% of your portfolio to a single "option"! Always manage your investments between different "options" to ensure better margins. Work out a plan where you know how to split your money between different stocks. Many people make the mistake of investing in the same stock assuming it will give them better results. This is all too common amongst novices and they will buy lots of stocks of a single good company. But doing so will only cause you to lose a lot of money, as there will be no space for risk. So plan out your investments before you delve into the stock market and allot just 5%, or less, to a stock, even if you think it is the best stock in the world!

Rule 6: New traders should always be careful and stay away from two emotions: 1. Greed: assuming that the price will go up further. 2. Fear: selling too quickly because you think the prices might dip. The bottom line is to remain level-headed and take decisions based on facts while trading. There are many novices that end up making this mistake and walk away with a measly profit. It will appear as a better option to exit when you are still in a little profit but it pays to wait on a good stock. You never know when it will pick up and keep moving forward. At the same time, panicking with a good stock's dip and deciding to take a loss on it will only cause you a lot of losses. Learn to be as intelligent as possible when it comes to trading with "options", or trading in general, in the stock market.

We have had a look at the very basics of day trading and now we will nose dive into it in much more detail. Starting in the next segment, you will read about stocks, the basics of the stock market, how it operates, the techniques and strategies used by day traders, how day traders forecast market conditions, getting started on the basics of day trading, risks to consider etc.

I hope you walk away with as much information as possible and use this book as a reference guide for day trading.

James Carnegie

Chapter 6

What Are Stocks?

Before we get down to understanding what stocks are, let us first look at what portfolio income means. The IRS recognizes three types of incomes viz. active income, passive income and portfolio income. Active income is what you earn by actively participating in a business or working at a day job. Say for example you work in a 9 to 5 job and earn $3,000 out of it. This means that you have actively earned that income and it is now your "active income".

The second type is known as passive income and includes all those incomes that you have not actively earned. So income earned through rent, through sales of your personal items, proceeds received through the sale of books etc. form your "passive income".

The third type is known as portfolio income. This can be described as anything that is not earned actively or passively and therefore, is earned through monetary investments. So all your shares, stocks, bonds and other such investments form part of your "portfolio income".

In previous years, earning a portfolio income was considered to be a rich man's cup of tea. There would be several rich businessmen who would understand what it takes to invest in the stock market and make huge profits out of their investments. They would have a large group of advisers who made their job easier. It was considered to be out of reach to the common man, as he had no access to the advice, let alone the stock market. However, with the "dotcom boom" in the late 1990s and early 2000s, the regular man was able to deal in the stock market and often ended up becoming rich over night. It was suddenly possible for anyone to buy and sell shares and make huge profits out of it. The trend saw a steady growth and within no time, hundreds of thousands of people around the world started trading in shares, which they bought and sold to realize a profit.

So what are these "shares" that people buy and sell? Well, here is a simple explanation for it.

A share, equity or stock is a stake in a company's profits and earnings. A share entitles its owner to have a certain claim over the company. So the more shares that a person possesses, the more of a claim he has on the company's profits. A stock is best referred to as a share in a particular company. So if I were to have 1,000 shares in a company then I will have that much claim over the ownership of that company. These shares are issued to the public and or employees of the company, and can be bought and sold by common people.

Many people get confused between the meaning of "shares", "equity" and "stocks" but all three mean the same thing and can be used interchangeably as has been done in this book.

Who Are Shareholders?

Now that you have a good idea about what stocks are, let us look at "shareholders" in detail.

Shareholders are all those people that hold the shares of a company. So say you hold 1,000 shares in Apple Inc. that will make you a shareholder in that company. Similarly, anybody who holds a stock, equity or shares in a company becomes its shareholder.

So as a shareholder of a company, you will have a share in everything that the company owns or is about to acquire. But the value of your stake in the company will be quite small compared to the entire gamut that the company owns. Say for example that the company is worth $1 billion. You own 1,000 shares in it. This will entitle you to just 0.01 percent of that value, if each share is worth $1, which can be considered a small portion. However, given how big the actual amount of the business is, you will also have quite a substantial amount to your credit.

But remember that not all companies will be worth that amount and there can be those that will be worth far less. But if you have more shares in a company that is worth a bit less, it is possible for you to match the same amount, as you would earn in having fewer shares in a richer company. So it can be regarded as being directly proportional and the "shareholders" stake in a company will depend on the total value of the shares that he or she possess and the actual worth of the company.

Back in the day, companies would issue a "stock certificate" by putting in the name of the shareholder, the company, the number of shares that he or she possessed, a seal of authenticity etc. It would be a matter of pride for the person to own such a certificate and they would display it for others to see. However, in this day and age, where computers rule the roost, you will not be handed a hard copy of this certificate and might not get to see it at all. The broker that is helping you out will maintain a copy of it himself and will buy and sell its rights depending on your instructions. This is advantageous as there is no risk of theft or loss and you do not have to personally, physically carry it with you every time that you wish to sell your stock. You can command your broker to deal with it and he or she will sell it with just the click of a button.

One misconception that most people have in terms of being "shareholders" is that, they assume they will sit on the member's board and have a say in everything that the business does. But like I said, it is a misconception and you will not have a say in anything that the business does. You cannot own shares in Facebook and tell its CEO Mark Zuckerberg to do something differently. You will only have a share in its profits or losses and not have a say in its functioning.

If you indulge in day trading, then you will hold the shares of a company for just a few hours and that will not entitle you to any benefits whatsoever.

The standard shares that are issued to the public are known as common shares or stocks and do not bestow the owner with any special rights and privileges. Preferred shares are those that are given to only the top-level personnel of the company and will bestow its owners with a few special rights. These people might have a say in the functioning of the business. More on this is discussed later in this book.

Who Is Best Suited for It?

The stock market is open to anybody who is interested in dealing with stocks. There is no particular group of people who can deal in stocks. But it is most suited for those interested in making the most out of their money and helping it grow exponentially. People who invest in stocks have the chance to increase the value of their money within a matter of a few days.

Most investors are people who have a good idea about the share market. They will be well aware of how the market functions and what they need to do in order to increase their money's value. It is well known that the market is quite volatile and it takes a certain amount of speculation to make predictions about the future.

It is possible for any layman to invest in the market but you need to consider your risks before you invest. Once you get the hang of it, you will be able to trade in stocks with ease. You will have to read on its functioning andto understand how it works. There is ample information provided in this book on both the stock market and Day Trading, which will give you a chance to make an informed choice.

So it is also possible for others to take part in dealing with stocks. From small business owners to students and housewives, there is a wide array of people who take up stock trading. It is not important for the person to be rich. As long as they have a little money to spare, they can start investing in the stock market.

It is also not important for the person to have studied finance. It is possible to seek advice from a qualified investor in order to make the decisions. The people can also do thorough research themselves before deciding to invest in certain stocks. The more that a person learns, the better they can invest. There are several websites that offer a comprehensive look at investing in the stock market.

What Is the Stock Market?

The stock market is a place where stocks are dealt with. These stocks are shares of companies. It is possible for you to buy these shares from the market. The stock market can be compared to a regular market. There are both buyers and sellers who are present here. These buyers and sellers will be looking to buy their shares from others or from the company itself and sell their stocks to other potential buyers. There are two types of stock markets, the first one being the physical market and the second being the virtual market.

Both these types are popular, with the former being a choice for traditionalists and the latter for new age traders. Let us look at each of these in detail.

Physical stock exchanges

These are places where the traders physically meet and deal in stocks. It consists of both buyers and sellers who agree upon a price before finalizing a deal. These people are brokers that are working in lieu of the investors. They will assemble in a building and have their investors on call. They will keep updating them on the market situation and as soon as they get the green light they will either sell or buy the stocks of the companies. Each broker is given a separate workstation consisting of a computer and a telephone. These computers are interlinked and help the traders communicate with each other. There are also giant screens where the stock position in the market will be updated from time to time. This will help them in keeping their investors up to date.

Some of the most famous stock markets in the world include the New York Stock Exchange (NYSE) and the Bombay Stock Exchange (BSE). The latter is based in New York and is said to be the most prestigious stock exchange building in the world. The system followed here entails the different members of the stock exchange asking their brokers to deal in the stocks. The broker will then make his way to the floor of the exchange where a "specialist" will assist the brokers in finding buyers or sellers who will agree on the same price.

The Bombay stock exchange on the other hand is said to be one of the nosiest stock exchange buildings in the world. It literally feels like a fish market where brokers shout at the top of their lungs in order to sell and buy shares.

Virtual market

Virtual markets are the opposite of physical markets. Here, there is no trading that takes place on the floor. The traders are available online and the person can deal with them virtually. Nobody will physically come into contact with each other and everything will be done through computers. This type is also known as over the counter markets (OTC). The most popular of this type is known as the NASDAQ. This exchange deals in stocks of big companies such as Microsoft, Dell and Intel, all of which were previously only dealt in the NYSE. The virtual markets are popular, as they are easy to access and give the investor a chance to be in direct touch with the brokers.

Primary and secondary markets

There are two types of exchange markets, namely the primary market and the secondary market. The primary market is where all the stocks are created and opened to the public (IPO) and the secondary market is where existing stocks are traded. These existing stocks have already been issued and are being traded as used stocks. The physical and virtual stock markets deal in the latter types of stocks.

Back in the day, there was no "Day Trading". The investors would have to wait for long periods of time for their stocks to be sold. There would be only a few brokers who would deal with stocks. But ever since the 90's this trend changed for good.

There is no more waiting for the broker to call back and it's nowpossible for them to deal with their stocks within a day. With the onset of NASDAQ trading, investors can buy the stocks or "options" in the morning and sell them by evening or night.

How Does It Work?

The stock market is said to be extremely volatile as there is no one time when the stock value will remain steady. These stocks are subject to market fluctuations and will vary in value over the course of a single day.

A very simple principle guides the stock market's functioning. Both the buyers and the sellers have a part in how the market functions.

When a stock is bought by a large number of people then its demand rises. When its demand rises, so does its price. But when the stocks are all sold in bulk then their price drops. So the demand and supply of the stocks is what helps in determining its value.

When there is high demand then the supply will start to exhaust. When this happens, the company decides to raise the price so that less traders and investors can afford it. But when all the stock is sold and there is more supply than the demand then its value will drop steeply.

It is impossible to predict when it will rise or drop, as people's minds are volatile. They might like one company today and another one tomorrow. So it becomes difficult to judge which company stock is good to buy today and which one isn't.

However, it is possible to speculate and understand the market trends. Say for example 500 people have decided to buy Apple stocks. This will indicate that there is going to be a rise in its price because of large demand. Another person will buy it when it is still affordable and decide to hold on to it until its price rises. Once it does rise, he or she will sell it off to another investor, who will hold on to it until its value rises further and then sell it off.

But if there are many of these buyers whom will all sell their stocks at the same time then the stock's value will decrease.

These fluctuations can occur in a single day or over the course of a few weeks or months.

The investors will consider whether the company is worth the price and then decide on buying the stocks. Here, the name and fame of the company will not matter much. There was a time when people considered stocks belonging to certain big companies as being the best investments, as they would always be in demand, but that is not always true. You might notice that there is a dip in the stock market value of Microsoft and that this dip is causing people to sell their shares before they go into losses. But some smart ones will decide to hold on to their stock and wait until the price rises again before they take a call on selling it or holding on to it.

Apart from buying and selling stocks, the company's profit levels are also determined by how much profit the company is making. All companies are required to declare their profits so that people show an interest in buying their stocks. Again, it will be difficult to predict which company a majority will choose to invest in. Saym for example that Coca Cola and Rolex both announce their quarterly profits and Rolex surpasses Coca Cola by just a little. Now you may think that people will flock to buy Coca Cola and sell their Rolex stocks but just the opposite might happen. So it is difficult to predict how investors will think.

Some terms to understand

Bullish market

A bullish market refers to one that is doing quite well. It indicates that the market is showing an upward trend. People are interested in investing in the market, as they assume the trend will continue the same way. The bullish market is meant to be a good market trend and will allow you to ring in a lot of profits. The term bullish comes from the term "bull". Just like how the bull attacks a prey by stooping down and lifting the prey with its horns, the market does the same by flinging the stocks upwards. But it is tough to know whether the markets will remain stable, when they are in the bullish state. It is best to take maximum advantage of the situation and book your profits when it enters the bullish state.

Remember that not all the stocks will be on an upward trend and there will be some that will still be down. It is safe to say about 10% of the stocks will remain down and the rest will be high. Depending on how the markets have been behaving, you will be able to say for sure when the markets will turn bullish. Remember that your share market will be affected by other share markets located all over the world and it is important that you understand the implications of these market fluctuations. The bullish market is considered to be a seller's market where everybody quickly disposes of their stocks in a bid to realize a quick profit from them.

Bearish market

The bearish market is one that is doing badly. It is one that shows a downward trend. The bearish market will not give you lucrative results and you will end up losing money if you participate in it. It is best that you avoid trading in the bearish market and wait for the market to get better.

The term bearish comes from the animal the bear. Just like how the bear attacks a person by swooping down and attacking the prey, the bearish share market swoops down and affects the stocks. Here too, it is difficult to predict whether the trend will continue or change. It is best to hold on to your stocks and not sell them. The market might change at any time.

However, it is best to buy stocks at this time. The bearish market is said to be a buyer's market. So people will buy more and more stocks, in a bid to accumulate them before selling them at a higher price. Here too, you must consider the world's markets. Read the news and you will know when a market will rise or fall. You must plan your investments based on your observations.

Bearish bar reversal

A bearish bar reversal occurs when today's highest is higher than the previous day's high and the current price is lower than the previous day's low. This happens to a stock and the price of the stock drops. So you have to look out for it and do whatever is right for you. If you think you can sell the stock off and remain in good profit, then do so. But if you can hold on to your stocks then so be it. Don't panic and sell all of it. You will have to check whether the stock has taken on a bullish bar reversal for sure, if you wish to sell your stocks. Not every drop in the price of share will indicate a bullish bar reversal so study the share carefully.

Bullish bar reversal

A bullish bar reversal refers to a situation where today's lowest price is lower than the previous day's low and the current price is higher than the previous day's close. This is a good thing as the price of the share will now be high. You can decide to dispose of it and come into a profit. However, if you think the price will rise higher given the stocks versatility, then you can hold on to it for longer. But you have to calculate it first to be sure.

Chapter 7

What Is Best to Trade?

When it comes to buying and selling stocks, it is entirely up to the investor to choose whatever he or she thinks will be a good investment. It is tough to generalize the type of stock that will suit everyone, as there is no one stock that fits all rule. However, here are the types of stocks that can be dealt with in the share market.

Company Stocks

Company stocks are those that are issued by the company to their employees and also to the public. Although top companies do not directly open up their shares for the public, employees who own the shares can sell them in the market. There are several multinational companies to choose from including Microsoft, Coca Cola, Intel, Apple

Inc., Nokia etc. You can choose a company that you think will help you increase the value of your investment. You will have to research the companies which are doing well and which ones aren't and choose to invest in them accordingly. But don't be in too much of a hurry to find the best stocks for you. Take your time and observe the trend for a few months. Once you establish a pattern, you can start buying the stocks of that company.

Commodities

The commodities market is where several types of commodities are bought and sold. These commodities can be of the following types:

Agricultural

Agricultural commodities are food items such as vegetables, fruits, pulses and other crops. Each commodity has a different price and depending on which crops are doing well, you can decide to invest in them. These commodities are ideal for day trading as they generally rise in value by the end of the day. Some of the most preferred commodities include potatoes, pulses, rice and sugar.

Metal

Metals are also a good market for investors. Metals such as copper, nickel, iron and lead all have a good market value. It is possible for you to trade in these metals and you will have to look for the ones that are doing well currently. You can choose to hold on to them for a specific period of time and then sell them before the deal's expiry date.

Industrial

Industrial solvents, chemicals and other such liquid commodities are also quite popular. They are in constant demand and command high prices. You can choose the ones that you think will fetch you a good price and invest in them.

Energy

Energy resources such as crude oil, petroleum, paraffin etc. are also traded. These are required to fuel your cars, used in cosmetics etc. and so, are in constant demand. You can choose the one that you think is in good demand and trade with them.

Livestock

Just like the other commodities, livestock is also traded on a daily basis in the stock market. These include, pigs, sheep etc. There are many factors that can affect their prices including weather conditions, diseases and also their market demand and supply.

These form the various types of commodities that you can choose from and You can purchase one type or diversify by purcashing several types.

Currencies

When it comes to day trading, it is possible for the investor to trade in currencies. As an investor, you have a lot of choices and flexibility to hedge your currency exposure to risk. FX options, as currency trading in the option markets is popularly known as, allow the same core hedging and trading strategies used when trading options on ETFs, stocks and indexes. The best and most straightforward way to remember what type of "option" you need to trade on is to focus on the base currency, or the first currency in every currency pair. The second currency in the pair is the quote currency, or the counter-currency. "Options" prices are typically derived from the base currency and are relative to the quote currency.

A USD-based currency pair (per USD) is available for the ten FX pairs. For instance, when you expect the US dollar to strengthen against the Japanese yen, you purchase YUK calls. In the inverse situation, when you expect the yen to strengthen against the US dollar, you purchase YUK puts.

It is up to you to decide what you think are best suited to trade with, depending on the resources you have at hand. You need not have an extensive knowledge on these products and only a little knowledge is enough for you to know if the products are worth investing in.

Index

Index trading refers to a type of trading where you bet on the index's rise and fall. Each sector of the stock exchange will have an index, which will take into account the prices of all the stocks that are listed under that index. Then by dividing it by the number of stocks present in the market you will get a certain number. Now all of these indexes are pooled and a final index is prepared which is the entire share market's collective index. Now you can "bet" on where the index will reach by the end of the day. For this, you must study the individual indexes such as the IT industry index, the consumer goods index etc. Once you think you know where the index will be by the end of the day, you can invest on it.

ETF

An ETF is also known as Exchange Traded Funds. These ETF's are like mini mutual funds that are traded in the market. Each ETF will have a combination of different underlying securities and these will be split into several small pieces. You can buy these in bulk and they can be traded on a daily basis. The main idea is to buy them at a low price and then dispose of them at a higher price. You have to understand that they are slow movers and you will have to buy them and wait for them to grow in value. These are much preferred as they will give you the advantage of a mutual fund but can be exchanged on a daily basis.

Bonds

Bonds are securities that are issued by companies and can be bought and sold to realize a profit. These bonds can come in several different forms and are explained below:

Government bonds

Government bonds refer to those bonds that are issued by the government. As you may know, the government requires funds from time to time and will ask you to pay forward. Once you do, they will issue you a bond that is valued much lower than its actual value. After it matures, you can collect the amount you paid along with an interest that they would pay you for it. If at any time you wish to sell the bond, then you can do so and you will get paid a higher amount for it. The government might also agree to pay you a certain percentage interest every month and you can capitalize on this opportunity to keep your money safe and also earn a profit from it. This form of investment is extremely safe as the government will not default on paying you your due money.

Agency bonds

Agency bonds are much like government bonds. They are run by companies that the government funds. So these can be counted as government bonds. They will pay you a great rate of interest on your investment. However, you cannot expect the same guarantee from them as you would from government bonds. You might have to invest a certain fixed sum as well. But given their success rate, they are a great option for all those looking to safeguard their money and also earn a certain rate of return on it. The same rules apply to agency bonds when you wish to liquidate them. You can sell them at a higher price or collect your sum and interest at the time of maturity.

Federal bonds

Your local governments issue federal bonds. Just like how the central government issues bonds, your local governments will do the same. You can buy these bonds at low rates and then hold on to them. You can sell them whenever you like and earn a higher income from it. These bonds will pay you more than what your government bonds will as your local government will not need a lot of money for a high scale project and it will be slightly low key. This type of investment will be much better than saving in the bank, which will pay you much less interest.

Corporate bonds

Corporate bonds refer to those that are issued by companies. As you know, multinational companies also require money for their projects. This money they will raise by issuing bonds to the public. They will agree to pay you back after a while and until such time, pay you a fixed rate of interest. You can sell these bonds for a profit at any time. But you must understand that these companies will not provide you with a guarantee like your government and federal government bonds. So it will be a risk that you will be willing to take. However, if you choose a big multi national company then you might hit jackpot. Not only will you get paid more but also win over their loyalty. They might be willing to give you shares in their company at a discounted rate, which will be a bonus for you. You can then sell these stocks at a later date and realize a big profit from it!

Zero coupon bonds

Zero coupon bonds are extremely popular owing to their ease of trade. They are extremely liquid and there is always a lot of demand for them. Now suppose a zero coupon bond is worth $500. When you buy it, they will issue it at $100 and ask you to exchange it for $500 in 2 years' time. So despite it being valued at $100 now, you will get back 4 times the value after exchanging it in 2 years' time. So not only will your money be safe, you will also be able to increase its value several fold.

Chapter 8

What Types of Stocks are there?

When it comes to company stocks, there are two types - common stocks and preferred stocks. Let us look at each type in detail.

Common stock

Common stock is the usual stock that is bought and sold in the market. The general public are exposed to it and they do not have to go to lengths to find some. They are easily available in the market and can be bought and sold with ease. In fact, when you hear people say they have stocks in a company, then generally they are referring to these stocks and they have probably bought them from the share market.

Common stocks are said to be the first choice of majority investors as the capital gain is extremely high. Now say for example you have a certain number of common stocks of a company and the company declares a huge profit. You will have a chance to avail your share of the profit due to the fact of having a share in the company. This share of your profit is known as a "dividend". You will not have the privilege of having a say in the functioning of the business, but the high rates of dividend that can be attained makes this type a winner. The stockholder will also have the chance to vote for a board member. However, these types of shares come with a huge risk. In case the company declares bankruptcy, all the preferred stock holders, creditors and other investors will be paid first and if anything remains after this money has been paid, the common stock holders will be paid as well. These stocks are non-transferable which means that their rights cannot be transferred by the owner to another person.

Preferred stock

Preferred stocks are premium stocks that are issued to the employees of the company. They might not have the same voting rights but the advantage is that they will get a fixed amount of dividend as long as the company exists. So there is no problem of getting low dividends if the company is not faring well, which is an issue with common shares. Preferred stocks are also almost risk-free as the shareholders will be compensated after the company goes bankrupt or liquidated. The assets of the company will be auctioned off and whatever is earned will be paid to the preferred shareholders. These stocks are also transferable which means the rights of the stock can be transferred to others. But note that this might be subject to the company's policies.

When it comes to trading with these stocks, you will have to take the help of a broker, as you might not be a member of the stock exchange. Information on brokers is provided later.

Who Are Brokers?

Brokers are people that are employed at the stock exchange. They are people that you need to consult if you wish to deal in stocks. These people are meant to help people buy and sell their stocks in the stock market. Now you may wonder as to why you cannot directly buy these stocks and sell them without having to go through a broker.

Well, the answer is simple. You have to be a member of the stock exchange in order to buy and sell shares. Usually, members are big companies that might themselves have their shares open to the market. It is ideal for individuals to choose brokers in order to deal in stocks.

It is best to have one broker dedicated to dealing with your stocks making sure he is available to you at all times of the day.

Brokers can be of two types, full service brokers and discounted brokers. Let us look at each in detail.

Full service brokers

Full service brokers are those that provide full service to the individuals. They are hired to help in predicting the markets and also advising on the best stocks to invest in. These brokers are generally quite experienced and capable of predicting the stock market. Their advice is sought because it is easy for the investor to trust their judgment and not have to put in individual effort to study market

trends. These brokers can also be instructed to buy and sell shares in lieu of the investor without having to consult them for every deal. These brokers will, however, charge a high price for their services. They will generally charge a percentage of the deal and it might be a large percentage.

These types of brokers were the only ones that were available back in the day and people had no choice. But with time, discounted brokers came along who can advise for about half as much as the other stock exchange brokers.

Discounted brokers

The other type of brokers that exist are known as discounted brokers. These will only do the job of buying and selling for the investor. They will not provide any advice on which stocks are good to invest in and do not predict the market. They will keep updating the investors on trends and issue buy or sell advice for the stocks when asked to. As was said earlier, these types of brokers became popular only after the "dotcom" boom in the 90's. These brokers do not charge a high fee and therefore are much preferred. They will charge a small sum for the service that they provide and are usually a small percentage of the deal value.

How to Choose the Best?

When it comes to choosing the right type of broker for your day trading work, you have to choose the best. You need someone that is capable of advising you correctly and also someone who will help speculate on the market.

For young first time investors, it is better to consider discounted brokers, as they will serve the purpose of buying and selling stocks. The idea is for the first timers to understand how trading works and gain firsthand experience of what needs to be done. Since most the trading will start and finish within one day, it will be a good platform for the newbie to understand how the market works. They will also not have to shell out too much money for the broker and it can all be done within a fixed budget.

Once you get the hang of it and have enough money to pay for a broker, you might decide to hire a full service broker to help you with your trading.

Remember that for day trading, you have to look for day trading brokers in particular. These are men who have dealt with a number of stocks over a period of time and are capable of buying and selling stocks at lightning speed. This is important when you have to deal in stocks within a single day. These day traders do not usually charge high prices and might charge just a few dollars for a few days of trade.

Remember that the best broker will help you save quite a bit of money within a day. For this, you have to choose someone who is well versed with what it takes to get the best deal for the investor.

Brokerage Accounts

When it comes to hiring a broker, they will ask you to deposit a certain amount of money that they can use to buy and sell your stocks. Some brokers will have a minimum amount that you will have to deposit in order for them to start trading in lieu of you. This minimum will depend on the broker. Most will settle for a sum between $500 and $1,000 but it depends.

Remember that this minimum balance has to be maintained otherwise the broker will not deal for you. Even if you are trying to withdraw this money for yourself in order to transfer to another account it won't be possible until the person adds in the balance amount to have the minimum balance.

Trading Without Brokers

You must understand that it is possible for you to trade without a broker. There are websites that allow you to register yourself and start trading. There are several advantages to going without a broker and they are as follows:

• The transaction costs are much lower compared to employing a broker

• You will have a chance to personally study the markets and learn from firsthand experience

• Many times, it becomes easy to blame the broker for a mistake and pin the blame on him for losses, but when the person deals with the stocks himself then he will learn from the experience of having faced a loss

• It is easier to trade without having to wait for the broker to respond and you will have a chance to sell or buy stocks as soon as you want to

All these reasons contribute towards making trading without a broker a better option for day traders and can be considered by you as well.

James Carnegie

Chapter 9

Day Trading - Getting Started

Now that you have learnt the basics of day trading, let us look at what you can do to get started as soon as possible.

Computer

The very first thing to do is to buy yourself a computer. If you already have one, it would still be advisable to have another one solely to conduct your trade operations. Many people make the mistake of having just one computer and trying to balance everything on it. This will make you get confused and have all your work mixed up. You have to make it a point to have two separate workstations: one for your trading and one for your regular work. It is ideal to have a desktop for your trading activities as you will have the chance to sit in one place and conduct trading. Having an office set up at home will motivate you to take it up seriously. So you can consider having a workstation in your room in order to get started with your trading. Just make sure there are not too many distractions around you. If a computer is bulky then consider buying yourself a handy tablet. The main aim is to have something that will allow you to download and operate the software, so, it does not matter if it is a computer or a tablet. The reason why most people make use of a computer is the ease with which they can operate it and also have a bigger screen to look at all the information.

Knowledge

The next thing to do is acquire as much knowledge on the topic as possible. It is understood that you have by now learnt the very basics of day trading, but it is important that you increase your knowledge base even further. Look at everything that there is on a particular subject and read as extensively as possible. Look at how risk is calculated and if you will be a good candidate to start day trading. You can read from trusted websites and also buy books that provide information on the subject. Remember that no information is enough when it comes to trading in the stock market. Try to be open to the idea of learning on a daily basis. Spend an hour every day learning something new about the market, as that will go a long way in ensuring that you have enough knowledge about the market and will do the right things, most of the time. Once you have garnered enough knowledge, you can move to the next step.

Website

It is important that you register with a company where you can buy and sell stocks. There are many online companies to choose from and you can choose the best. Once you register, they will help you download the software that is required to buy and sell stocks. You will need special software for it, which is only available with these websites that trade stocks. The software will allow you to look at the stocks that are up for sale and with the click of a button andbuy or sell them. Most of this software is downloaded onto your computer but some might send across their technicians in order to download the software into your computer using CDs. Once the software is up and running, you can start trading, but before you do, consider the next step. Before you sign up, check the brokerage fee that the company will charge you. All companies charge their customers a certain percentage depending on the volume of the trade. There are some that will charge you less and those that will charge exorbitantly. You must know to choose the best one. Do a quick online search and look up companies that others have recommended. If you think the company charges a nominal value, then stick with them. Remember that the company will charge you brokerage regardless of you trading by yourself or availing the help of a broker.

Mind

Remember to prepare yourself mentally before you start day trading. You have to realize that day trading is extremely risky and you will have to prepare yourself for profits or losses. You have to make up your mind to have a firm head on your shoulders so that you don't lose your cool and end up making the wrong decisions. It is natural to be angry at times but you have to remain calm for the majority of your trading time. You must try and remain alert and not be distracted by something. Make sure you are energized and not feeling weak as you will need quite a bit of brain power while trading, especially if you are using the scalping technique to trade. Remember to leave your emotions outside the door. Many people end up making mistakes by getting emotionally attached to a stock. Tell yourself before trading that you will not get emotionally attached to any stock or company and will tread carefully in the market.

Observe

The next step is to familiarize yourself with the software that you are using for your trading. Remember that you need to know everything that there is to about the software including its operation and how it works. If you start without understanding the basics, then you will find it very difficult to trade. Next, observe the market trends keenly. You can look at the stock prices and look for the ones that are doing well. Each type of stock or security will have a trend graph, which will give you an idea of how it has been faring in the past. You will have an idea of whether it is going to rise in value or drop and if it is a good idea for you to invest in it. You can look at all the commodities, securities and stocks and then decide on which ones to invest in.

Brokerage

Many times, you will start to feel overwhelmed and may not know where to start. This is especially true for beginners, as they will not have an idea of what to do to start with trading. If after repeated attempts, you are not able to understand what is best for you then you can consider consulting a broker. As was explained before, brokers are middlemen who help people in investing in the stock market. It is possible for you to hire one at any time and they will help you out. You will have to contact one and set up a brokerage account. You must then transfer money and ask them to help you in understanding how it works. After they trade a few stocks for you, you will have a good idea of how it works and garner the confidence to do it by yourself. If you are confident enough, you can stop using the service provided by a broker entirely.

Buy

When it comes to buying the stocks or securities, you must buy them in bulk. It is not possible to buy one or two stocks. There will be a minimum purchase amount that will be mentioned next to the stock value. Remember that you have to make a minimum investment when you buy stocks and this minimum will differ from company to company. It will also differ from website to website and so, you must look at the minimum amount that needs to be invested in order to buy stocks for day trading purposes. If you are choosing "options", then you will have to pay an advance towards the stocks or securities that you wish to reserve.

Wait

Once you have bought the stocks, it is advisable for you to wait. As was mentioned earlier, you have to let the first hour pass. After that, you will have a clear idea of where the stocks are headed. If you feel that they are rising then all is well. If they are falling, don't panic - they might rise again by the end of the trading day. Make sure you are observing the trend carefully at regular intervals. Those who take up day trading as their main job are required to spend time in front of their computers and look at the trends all through the day until the trade for the day closes. If you don't have the time to do this, then considering the services provided by a broker is a good idea.

Sell

The next step is to sell all your stocks and securities. This is done by the end of the day. Selling is also known as liquidating and for options it is known as liquidating your position. Remember that you have to sell your stock on the same day in order for it to be called day trading. If you hold on to your stock overnight, then it will be known as regular trading. Once you sell it, you will have a chance to make a profit. Your profit will be deducted from the value of the stock at the time of purchase and transferred to your account. But remember that you must invest wisely and make sure that you are coming into good profit before deciding to buy and sell stocks and securities. There are many techniques for buying and selling using speculation and they are explained in detail in the next segment of this book.

Record

Remember to always maintain a detailed record of your transactions. You will have to make a record of it and have it readily available. You will need it for future reference and try to maintain both a hard copy and a digital copy. You can also take a screen shot and append it with your records. Having a detailed report helps you gauge your profits and losses and gives you a chance to predict a pattern that you will follow with your buying and selling. It is ideal to go through the entire month's data at the end of the month. If it is possible, then try to get working notes of someone who has found a lot of success in the stock market. Maybe you will find some valuable information there, which you can use to your advantage. Go through it in detail and see if there is anything that you should do or avoid doing to bring in profits.

Repeat

Once you get the hang of it, you will know to repeat the processes. You will fall into the habit of buying stocks, selling them and recording the transactions. After a while, you will start looking at it as a mundane activity and set yourself up for a bright career in day trading. But remember to remain cautious and do things that will benefit you in the long term as well as in the short term.

Message boards

Message boards refer to the online communities where you can look at suggestions that are given by other experts. Many times, you will find that good stocks have been mentioned and you can trade in them. However, don't blindly follow everything that you read here. Do your research before deciding on the stocks of a particular company. If you think the company is good, then invest in it but if you think the message board is getting it all wrong then stay away from the stocks.

Watch list

Once you create your account, you must also create your watch list. A watch list is one where you add the names of all the stocks that you wish to trade. Trying to look at them individually will waste your time. So it is best to have all of them in one place and go through them on a daily basis. You can add in as many companies as you like and can also create separate watch lists. Since it is day trading, it is best that you delete your previous watch list and start afresh on a day-to-day basis.

These form the various steps that you can adopt to get started on your day trading activities. But remember that this is just a suggestion and if anything is working well for you then you can carry on with it.

James Carnegie

Chapter 10
Techniques and Strategies Used in Day Trading

By definition intraday trading refers to the practice of buying and selling stocks on the same day. So if you have purchased a stock in the morning you have sold it off before the end of the market hours on the same day and closed of all your positions. You will not carry over a trade to the next day. To a certain extent, you will start afresh each day, do not carry over the burden of the previous days losses, nor the euphoria of a win.

There are two distinct opportunities while trading that is you buy first and then sell for a profit, or you sell first and wait for the market or stock to come down and then book your profits. This technique is called going short or shorting. As a novice, we recommend that you buy first and then sell, and the shorting technique can be used as you scale up and become more proficient.

Let us look at Day trading or intraday trading as it is called in more depth in terms of the techniques and strategies. While doing your extensive studies on the numerous studies available in the markets, it is near impossible to follow or adopt all of them. So the trick is to, adopt a maximum of 3 – 4 studies that you think are the best fit to your temperament and which suit your style. There is no right or wrong path to take in choosing a style, hence do not compare your style with styles or strategies adopted by other more successful traders. What works for them may or may not work for you and vice versa. It is absolutely imperative that you focus on your level of comfort and stick to the same. It takes a lot of self-discipline and control to hold on to the values that are intrinsic to you.

Once you have identified the studies, techniques and strategies, write them down in your personal diary and look at them and read them out aloud every day before starting to trade at the beginning of the day and at the end of the trading day.

I also suggest that you write down your goals in terms of what you are hoping to achieve from this exercise that you have undertaken. Do read out aloud the goals as recommended above. The power of mind and repetition has its own benefits and will reap you huge benefits not only in your endeavor but also in all walks of life. There are two primary schools of thoughts for intraday trading:

1)   You treat it is as a serious and full time business

2)   You are considering it as a parallel source of income, along with your regular job (you need to be serious here too)

While this book will attempt to cover both, choose one that suits your style. Let us begin with the former that you treat it as a full time job or as your own business.

Having said that, there are a few precursors to the same. It takes a lot of grit and determination on one's part to adopt this as a full time business.

If you are fresh out of college or young, where there are few responsibilities on your shoulders, it would be advisable to make it your full time occupation as you have time on your side.

Alternatively, if you are already holding a job, and have the responsibility of your family to take care of, one would advise to begin by doing it part-time and once you become an expert then take the leap of faith and quit your job and enter into it full time. A dream come true for many.

So without further ado, here are a few pointers that have to be at the top of your list.

1)   Self-discipline

2)   A strong psychological profile

3)   Following a set of pre-defined rules

4)   Keep updating your knowledge

5)   Adapt and be flexible

Intraday is not for the faint hearted. The volatility of the markets is not for everyone, so if you are the kind of person who panics easily at the first sign of volatility, probably intraday trading is not your cup of tea. So the question to ask then is, 'If intraday is not for me, then what do I do'?

Well there are other styles of trading which may suit your personality like swing trading, or long term trading which are covered later on in this book.

You could also learn the art of becoming a calm and composed person. There are various programs that will help you attain the same. Once you realize the power of self-control, and are confident enough to be calm during tremors, you can then take up intraday full time.

If you are endeavoring to take up intraday as a full time profession, it is advisable to be in front of the trading terminal or your computer during market hours contrary to the second school of thought which advises that you need not be in front of the trading terminal at all times. If you have ever seen intraday traders at their trading desks, you will see multiple screens in front of their faces, at times up to four screens. We recommend that you have at least two screens as a beginner, one for your market watch (covered later in this book) and one for you to actually execute your trades, which are your buy and sell orders.

You will also need to analyze your trades during after-market hours, so that you are prepared with a plan well in advance before the dawn of the next market day.

What is it that you analyze during after-market hours? Again there are two schools of thought:

- Fundamental Analysis

- Technical Analysis

Fundamental Analysis: covered in brief in the latter part of this book, is quite tedious and difficult and requires years of experience and teamwork to get to the bottom of it. It is best left to the experts (unless now that you have taken up this up full time, you take the onus of the various studies like balance sheets, profit and loss account, cash flows and income statements of all the companies that you are interested in trading in), in which case if you are going to use fundamental analysis for trading, you are better off hiring a full time broker *(whose charges are quite expensive)* to provide you with the information on the fundamentals of a company, based on which you would take a judgment call and then trade accordingly. Mind you, while the broker will provide the information, the profit or loss aspect of the trade is entirely yours and the broker does not hold any responsibility for the same in spite of the expensive charges.

Technical Analysis: also known as charting, is widely used worldwide and we recommend that you study technical analysis as a base for venturing into the world of intraday trading. Technical analysis is also a wide and extensive subject and within technical analysis, the candlestick pattern study has more acceptance and recognition. Essentially what technical analysis does is based on the past history of the market data - predominantly the price and volumes - and it develops a method for anticipating the general course that the price will take on any time frame. Time frames are candlestick chart studies that can be done on a monthly, weekly, daily, hourly, you can even drill down to 120 minutes, or 60 minutes or 30 minutes to even as low as 1 minute charts.

We will provide a brief description on this aspect that is the candlestick patterns. While the study of candlestick and its patterns again is an enormous learning; the good news is that you do not need to invest four years in a college or university to obtain the same. Either you can carry out a self-study using the vast repertoire of knowledge available on the Internet or search for a program being conducted by some experts or financial institution in your area. The investment would be well worth your time.

Once you are through with your studies, the next step is to obtain software that provides you with the candlestick software and real time analysis of the stocks during market hours. With the advent of technology, most of the good brokerages have nowadays invested in developing such software. Identify a broking firm that will serve multiple purposes (having an online broking firm bodes well, so that you can reap the benefits of a good broking firm, from the confines of your home), so that it will provide you with the software for analysis as well as execution of trades and also charge you a minimal brokerage fee. This works well in your favor since you would have a single point of contact for all your needs.

While the basic software for candlesticks will throw up the different types of candles, it is up to you based on your study, to spot the different patterns and their applications in your trades. There is more sophisticated software available which may be able to spot the patterns, and which can be customized to spot other parameters based on the rules that you have defined for yourself. This software is usually available at a premium. A word of caution, this software just provides the analysis and predictions. The markets though may behave in a completely irrational manner, and you will be left wondering what happened.

What causes the markets to behave in an irrational manner? This depends on various factors, like the global economy, fluctuations in the currencies, GDP data of a country and the company quarterly results to name a few. Do your research on other factors that affect the markets either in a positive or negative way and then trade accordingly. It is advisable not to trade in a company whose results are going to be announced on that day as the volatility may swing any way and you would be caught unawares in spite of the studies and analysis. Once you have gained more experience and graduated from being a novice, you can then trade on these days also, as the impulsiveness on these days is huge, and you have a better chance of making a handsome profit.

Similarly, when important government announcements are made which may affect a particular sector, this is turn may affect companies in that sector. Be wary of trading in the days prior to the announcements or on the day of the announcements as the markets will factor in uncertainty and other unknown parameters and could swing either way contrary to your analysis. Learn to link and apply news that you read to your trading strategy. For example, if the government allows a policy decision favoring the automobile sector, then you know that the stocks in these sectors are going to rise and vice versa if the decision is not in the favor of the automobile sector then the stocks in this sector are going to go down. These kinds of decisions cause the analysis to fail and once you learn the art of spotting these, you will be able to take better trading decisions.

Maintain a calendar of these important events and try and do paper trading during these days as a beginner.

Paper trading is the process of doing simulation trading where websites offer you the option of trading as per the markets but you are not trading with real money, rather with dummy currency. You can derive your profits or loss that you would have made had you actually used your trading account. You cannot cash in on any profits made using paper trading but neither will you incur any loss in paper trading. There are numerous websites that offer these services, ask around and pick one that has been around for some time and has got a reputation of being stable. www.warriortrading.com for example, offers the services of paper trading.

To avoid the above pitfalls, it is good to be abreast of current financial news on a global level. A useful website is www.tradingeconomics.com. There are several others so take your pick.

When you are trading intraday, during market hours, reserve a place in your home as your workspace. Ensure that it is free of all standard distractions, treat it the way you would at work. Trading intraday is a discipline, and we recommend that you start small and work your way up. Prepare yourself so that you will start seeing substantial difference in your trading and profits, only as time goes by and this could be as long as one year. Do not get disheartened in the beginning if you lose money - in fact, be prepared for it. Set aside a budget for your intra day trading and decide on the acceptable loss that you are willing to incur on a daily basis across trades. Once you hit this loss, stop trading for that day and walk away from the terminal, shut down your computer _ tomorrow is another day. Do not make the mistake of investing more money on that day and try to time the markets, you may end up making more losses than ever.

The rationale behind this is that, on some days things will just not work the way you want to, and this is not restricted to trading alone, you may have experience this somewhere along the way in any sphere of life. Remember that you do not control the markets, it has a mind of its own and the sequence will unfold through the day.

In intraday or in any other style of trading you are dealing with probability. Remember always: there is no sure fire winning formula -you always will be dealing with a probability. The trick is to try and tilt the probability in your favor using a combination of studies, markets, technical analysis that you have done so far and will continue to do on a consistent basis for you to be a successful trader.

When you try to tilt the probability in your favor, what is an optimal ratio that one should target? Studies say that a 70:30 ratio in your favor is more than enough for you realize your profits. So if you take 100 trades in a month and if 30 of them go wrong, but 70 trades swing your way, you will have made decent profits. And I use the term decent profits, not handsome profits. The handsome returns will come with time as the quality of your trades increase with more knowledge and fine tuning of that knowledge to suit your requirements. The different ratios along with the number of trades are defined in this book in the latter section. Feel free to choose which suits you best.

While the above may seem like a lot of theory, it will set the tone for you to keep realistic expectations, rather than speculating and depending on hearsay. The worst mistake people make when entering the stock markets is depending on other people to do their work for them. A friend's uncle living in Timbuktu provides a tip that the stock of company X will do well and will rise. Based on this you take a trade in company X, and to your bad fortune the stock tanks and you end up burning you fingers. You then take a decision that the stock market is not for me and decide to quit. While there is nothing wrong with quitting while you are making an informed decision, leaving the markets because of misinformation is a fallacy, as you will have given up on your chances of being self-independent in terms of monetary aspect.

Realize one thing, that if you are entering the stock markets for any kind of trading, you only depend on yourself and your studies. While discussion among peers is healthy, it is for you to research the advice, rather than blindly following it, to save heartburn later on.

Coming back to the 70:30 ratio, the next thing to tackle is the reward to risk ratio of a particular trade. So what is a reward to risk ratio, it is the risk you are willing to take to garner a certain reward. The ideal situation or studies denote that on an intraday trade a ratio of 1:2 is good enough. That is for every 1$ that you lose the profit should be 2$. If the stock you are analyzing does not offer you the risk to reward ratio of 1:2, then ***DO NOT TAKE THE TRADE***. Do not be obsessed with only one script, move on to some other stocks and analyze those, until you find a couple of them which will provide you with the desired opportunity of 1:2 risk to reward ratio.

Let us demonstrate this with an example of a hypothetical company called ABC Inc.

Current Market price of ABC Inc. = 10 USD

Your buying price of ABC Inc. = 10 USD

If the stock rises you sell, at lets says 14 USD, so the profit you have made from this is 4 USD (*after brokerage and other tax angles)

If the stock falls you stop your losses at $8, that is you sell off the stock for $8 and incur a loss of $2. Hence, the rewards to risk ratio in this case would be $4/$2 that is 2:1. As you become more proficient over time, you can increase the reward to risk ratio to 3:1. Make sure that you set a rule that when the reward ratio touches 3 you will book your profits and exit the trade no matter what. This involves the psychological aspect of human nature that is greed. If you wait for the Rewards ratio to increase, the contrary might happen and you risk losing your capital as well. Of course the stocks could still rise and if you are confident of your studies and are sure that the rewards ratio is going to go higher than 3, then you can book your profit in tranches. Again logic says that a trade should be exited in a maximum of three tranches, though this can vary from individual to individual.

Tranches is the process in which you sell off your stocks, or book profits in your stocks in phases. For example, if you hold 100 stocks of ABC Inc., and when you reach the reward ratio of 2:1 you sell off 50 shares, which means you have already booked your profit and regained your capital. As a professional you will now move up your stop loss from the original ratio of 1 (that is at $8 as per above example, to $14), so even if the stock does not reach the reward ratio of 3:1 it will hit your stop loss of $14 and you will book out at a profit. If, however, your stock does reach the reward ratio of 3:1, you sell off another tranche of shares – let's say 30 shares move your stop loss upwards from $14 to $16 and then book out the last tranche of 20 shares as the stock rises or hits the new stop loss of $16. This concept is also known as trailing stop loss.

Prior to executing any trade, ensure that you have done your analysis completely based on the studies and chart patterns. Once you are confident that you are ready to execute a trade, make sure that you have written down or stored somewhere the following three important parameters.

Buying price: This is the price at which you will purchase one or multiple units of shares in a company.

Target Price: This is the price at which you will sell one or multiple units of shares in a company. (Refer to the trailing stop loss section above)

Stop Loss Price: This is the price you will exit at from the trade, should the markets not go as you had anticipated. This is the all-important safety mechanism that you must have. Most professional traders will never ever trade without a stop loss in place. This risk management is an essential part of your trade management as even a perfectly defined strategy can go wrong at times. This will safeguard your losses to a minimum at the same time as guaranteeing that your capital is not eroded completely. The stop loss has to be entered into the system and not just in your mind.

Intraday trading can give every individual the kind of outlook that they are looking for. If you are the kind who craves excitement, it will give you the exhilaration during fast trades, or trades that you cover in a very short period of time. Just to give you a heads up, some of the intraday traders trade within a span as short as 3 to 5 minutes. To do this, you have to have your trade management plan ready and need to be computer savvy to operate the software that punches in the three different prices which were mentioned above.

All it takes is practice and with time, you too will be able to make fast trades. The advantage of fast trading is that you make multiple small profits throughout the day.

If you are the kind of person who has a more laid back approach and attitude, then intraday trading is definitely not for you. Instead,you should adopt a different style like swing trading or long term trading, wherein you do your analysis, plan your trade management, punch in the prices and then sit back and monitor the prices on a day to day basis to check if they are travelling the path that you have anticipated. If not, timely correction and revision to the price should be made.

It is also important for you to set aside working capital for your intraday trading. Again this will vary with person to person. Invest only what you feel comfortable with. Do not take a loan to start off your trading, as if things can go seriously wrong you will further fall into the debt trap.

You credit your trading account with $25,000. This is the minimum account required as per US equities market. You then need to calculate the percentage risk per trade withthe recommendation here being 0.50%, which works out as 1,250$. There are other firms called Prop firms which will allow you to invest below the 25.000 mark that you can join with a $5,000 membership fee   the setback to these firms is that they generally charge a higher commission than your regular trading brokerage firms, and they also may or may not take a percentage of the profits. A prop firm will allow traders who do not have the initial investment of $25,000 to join at a membership fee of $5,000. You will be trading with the firm's money as if it is your own money. You will be issued a 1099 tax form annually for calculation of profit or losses.

As a rule of thumb, 30% of your working capital should be in intraday and 70 % in long-term trades from the outset. As you move from being a novice to an expert over a period of time, the ratio can gradually keep changing till it reverses completely. That is, 70% of your capital should now be in intraday, so that you have more capital to invest and reap your profits accordingly. As your profits and capital grows, so does the position size of your trades, while initially in the early days you may have traded with 15, 20, 50 or even 1 share or stock of good companies, this number will go up as your position size increases.

Use the above as an example only: the percentage can be varied as per your level of comfort and the risk value calculated accordingly. Have a reward system for successful trades, do not penalize yourself for unsuccessful ones. Rather, analyze what went wrong. If after a few trades, you find that you are repeating the same mistake again and again, it's time to change track, and adopt a different strategy. This will definitely take your trading skills up anotch. Intraday trading is like climbing a ladder: you get to the top rung-by-rung, one rung at a time.

It is also important to consider the tax angle on your trades. If you make trades with a small Rewards to Risk ratio, two things will happen:your profits can quickly erode with factors like tax, brokerage fees and any other charges. Secondly if you keep the risk ratio too lowm you will find that with small fluctuations in the market you are hitting the Stop Loss Price too often and are exited automatically from the trade by the software. Please refer to the risk to reward ratio explained above.

Note: You will have to pay the broker a brokerage for every trade that you take, the broker does not take into account whether you are booking a profit from the trade or incurring a loss from the trade, and he will extract his pound of flesh regardless.

Take advice from a good tax consultant who will be able to guide you on your tax eligibility, as this could again vary from individual to individual.

During the duration of the day or market hours, do not make more than 2 – 3 trades per day. You would have arrived at the plan well in advance that is a day before to determine the stocks that you are going to trade in. To arrive or narrow down to those 2 – 3 trades per day, you will have to analyze close to 100 stocks per month. It is time consuming, but it is a study that can be conducted after market hours, one need to have the patience and due diligence to carry out the same.

While candlestick patterns form the basis of your analysis, these need to be supported by other parameters or studies.

As mentioned before, there many of them available, in addition to hundreds of books by respected authors. Below, we list a few studies that you will need to do in juxtaposition to the candlestick patterns to authenticate your decisions:

- Moving Average

- Multiple Time Frames

- Trends

- ATR or average true range

- Support and Resistance

- Fibonacci ratios

Once you start applying the above studies to your trades, and if all of them point in a similar direction, then you can be assured that these are authentic indicators, which will supplement your candlestick analysis, thus tilting the probability in your favor.

Create your own set of rules, start off by creating a laundry list of rules that you are accustomed to. By the process of elimination arrive at approximately 15 to 20 rules that you think will work to your advantage. Then eliminate them further till you are left with no more than 10 rules in your kitty. Once you have whittled down to these 10 rules, consider them to be sacrosanct and do not break even one of them while executing a trade. Most of the losses that you make in the markets, if you look back and evaluate them, you will realize that they took place because you broke one or multiple rules of your own, while taking the trade.

Once you start applying the rules to all your trades, it will eventually become a habit. There will be days when you are stuck and will be left with stocks that do not conform to the studies and rules, or are contrary to the studies and analysis done by you. Do not be stubborn and trade on these days for the sake of trading. In all eventualities, you will end up breaking a rule or set of rules and end up incurring a huge loss. When such a situation arises, take a step back, and stay calm. Go back to the drawing board and start further analysis for the next day. You are bound to come up with stocks that will meet the standard requirements and conform to you set of pre-defined rules.

As a day trader you can also use a concept called margin trading or leverage, which means you are trading with borrowed money from the broker. The ratio of leverage is generally 4:1. For example if you have the power to invest $5,000 ,you will be given $20,000 to trade with. If you purchase shares at $100, you would purchase 200 shares of a company X. If the stock goes up by $10 a share, you will make a profit of $2,000. However, if the stock goes down by $10 and you have to square off your position by the end of the day, your risk losing $2,000from your initial capital of $5,000. Hence margin trading is not advised for beginners. Once you develop the habit of winning trades consistently you can work with margin trading.

The first 15 minutes of the market are suspect to high volatility. A word of caution for those stepping out as rookies: avoid trading in the first 15 minutes. Once the dust settles down, you can begin to act on your plan. As with everything else, you can move to the first 15 minutes of trading after you get the hang of trading daily.

As mentioned earlier, do not trade based solely on tips received from uniformed sources, or friends, and in the case that you do receive tips, analyze them as per your set criteria and rules, and only then initiate a trade.

Important things to remember in intra day trading are listed below:

1.   Set your prices into the system for stop loss, target and buy.

2.   Trade only in 2 – 3 stocks at any point of time on any given day

3.   Realize your profits when you meet your targets and do not fall prey to the human emotion of greed by waiting for the stock to go up more.

4.   Use the trailing stop loss concept in continuation to point no 3.

5.   Choose stocks based on your studies and only those that can provide you with the Rewards to Risk ratios mentioned above.

6.   If you are having a bad day, do not try and fight the markets, instead shut down your system and walk away before incurring more losses before starting afresh the next day.

7.   Maintain a watch list and monitor it daily, so that when a stock approaches, your studies and analysis will tell you when to take the trade.

8.   Start small as a beginner and scale up as you become more experienced with time.

9.   Update your knowledge continuously

10.   Be flexible and adaptable

This in short is the crux of intra day trading.

Swing Trade Mechanism

The swing trade mechanism is another technique used by day traders. It involves holding the stock for some time but since it is used in regular trading, some question its application in day trading. Swing trading can be a great option for day traders as it allows them to swing between positions at the same counter. Here, the trader will re-enter into a fresh position from the same counter in case a stop loss comes by. Now say we take into account the same example as before. Once the trader liquidates the position, he will again open a fresh position in the same counter. If the value of the stock then rises to $475, then he will make a profit of $50, which will help him in making back whatever he lost. If it rises to $485 then he will have a $10 profit and so on and so forth.

These are the two mechanisms that will help you get started with day trading, but now let us look at the strategies that are adopted, in detail.

Trend Following

This is the most important strategy to be considered when it comes to day trading. Remember, the time frame within which you have to make your choice is very small. In fact, it is not any more than a few hours and so you will have to be as smart with your choices as possible. The trend following technique is where the trader will observe the instruments that are rising and falling. He will assume that the ones that are rising will continue to rise and the ones that are falling will continue to fall. If he has stocks of the ones that are rising, then he will hold on to them and also buy new stock. He will also simultaneously avoid the declining ones and short sell the ones that he has in his position in order to prevent any loss. This is probably the best strategy for day trade beginners.

Contrarian Trading

As was said earlier, the time frame for buying and selling day trade stocks is very short. You will have to make a decision within a short period of time. In the previous strategy, the investor was optimistic with the rising stocks and pessimistic with the declining ones. But in this strategy, the trader will adopt a contrary view. He will be optimistic of the falling stocks and pessimistic with the rising ones. That is, he will decide to quickly sell off the rising ones assuming that it will begin to fall and buy more of the declining ones by assuming that they will start to rise. This technique can be quite risky but if it turns out to be true then it will help the trader make a lot of profit. However, if you are a beginner, then it is ideal to wait until you have had a little experience before attempting to use this strategy.

Candlestick Patterns

The "candlestick" pattern is best suited for people who would like to adopt a technical approach and trade based on patterns and predictions. The "candlestick" pattern involves the creation of patterns for particular stocks based on its "LOD" or lowest of the day and "HOD" or highest of the day prices. Depending on these statistics, the graph is plotted. There is a technique known as the doji reversal pattern that helps in establishing proper "candlesticks". Once the "candlesticks" have been established, the trader will be able to identify the pattern that the stock will follow. Once it has been established, he will predict whether the price will rise or plummet. Depending on the prediction the trader will decide to either hold on to the stock or sell it off. This technique is easy to follow if you understand the technique properly and for that, you can research the topic further.

Rebate Trading

Rebate trading is a good option to beginners who wish to see a good profit within a few months of starting their trading careers. Rebate trading is possible only through electronic communication networks. These are online service providers that help people invest. When a person wishes to invest through ECN's, he or she has to pay a certain commission in order to avail of the service. These ECN's thrive on these commissions and they are what make it possible for them to function optimally. But these ECN's will require investors who will create a market for them. This market is created by people who invest in a large number of shares and involves both buying and selling. When a trader buys or sells a large volume of stocks that are priced low, then the ECN will pay a commission. This commission coupled with the small profit will prove to be quite lucrative for the trader. This therefore, will prove to be a good opportunity for newbies to start day trading.

Range Trading

Range trading as the name suggests, deals with trading within a fixed range. This range consists of highs and lows. The high is the highest high that the stock can reach and the low is the lowest that it can reach. The range trade rule believes that the price of the stock will hit high and then rapidly fall to its low and once it falls low it will rise high again. This will help in establishing an average price line, which will make the pattern predictable. The trader will sell the stocks that are about to go high and buy the ones that are going low. This will help in making a profit out of his trade. This system is a lot like the trend following system except that the trader is sure of the outcome and is not merely guessing it.

Price Action

It is no secret that the main thing involved in a stock market is "price fluctuation". It is the rise and fall of the stock prices that makes it possible for the trader to break into a profit, or suffer a loss. So to remain successful, the trader has to predict the price rise and fall successfully. This can be done through a method known as price action. Price action is conducted by taking into account the various prices that the stock has held over a period of time along with other data, statistics and mathematical formulas that are applied in order to arrive at the price fluctuation rate and range. This will help the trader make accurate speculations and realize profit whilst minimizing losses. However, as good as it sounds, the formulas that are used are extremely complex and the average person might not be able to do it easily.

Scalping

Scalping is an advanced method to adopt and will help in making instant profits. The trader here is meant to be extremely proficient and understand the trends that the market follows. Scalping is a technique that is used to enter into a position and then immediately sell it within a matter of minutes. It sounds almost impossible but in fact it is very possible. Here, the trader will know exactly when the price will change. He will be just so accurate that the very minute that he decides to liquidate, the price would have risen. So it is literally scalping the stock and running away with a profit. But for this to happen, the trader should be well versed with the market's functioning. Say for example he buys 10 stocks of $1,000 each; he will then immediately sell them within a few minutes when they have risen to $1.500 each. This will give him an instant profit of $5,000. Again, you will have to have at least 3 to 5 years of experience in order to adopt this day trading technique.

AI Trading

Ever since computers are used to help in trading, there has been one technological improvement after another, all of which have caused trading to turn into an electronic gamble. It is believed that nearly 1/3 of the trading population relies on predictions that are calculated by computer-generated algorithms and all that the trader does is wait for it to come up with a result. These automatic algorithms are extremely accurate and therefore, everybody will buy and sell stocks that are profitable. This has only lead to immense competition in the trading arena, which makes it a bane to several traders. It is believed that depending on artificial intelligence has also affected the profit levels and people are now dealing with reduced profits for the stocks that they buy and sell. So don't over-rely on these to help you pick the stocks. You need to understand the downside of something before you decide to make it your full time strategy.

News Forecasts

It was previously mentioned in this book that apart from the buying and selling of stocks, a company's profitability also affects its stock value. So, say for example that a company announces that they are undergoing losses and might not pay dividends;in this situation, it is wise to sell off their stocks at the earliest. On the contrary, if they announce that they are doing extremely well then it is wise to hold on to their stocks and perhaps even buy more. So the news of whether the company is faring well or not will help in determining the trader buying or selling his stocks. But, remember that before the official announcement from the company, there will be rumors that will be doing the rounds. This will be enough for some traders to base their judgment upon and you must check the prices of the stock regularly to understand whether the rumors have had an impact on the value of the stocks.

The above, form the various strategies that traders adopt in order to indulge in day trading. But here, it is also very important to understand the techniques that traders use in order to forecast the fate of stocks. We will look at these in detail in the next segment.

Chapter 11

Understanding The Stock Market

When it comes to understanding the stock market, there are many things to look into. Starting with the type of company, the value of the share etc. To make it easier for you to understand there are three types of analysis that you can conduct so that you know what the best shares to buy are. In this segment, we will look into the technical, fundamental and contrarian view of stock buying.

Technical

The technical view of a stock is seen as an important aspect to consider. As you know, a company's shares will rise and fall throughout the day, day in and day out. Right from the time of its inception, the share will set a pattern that it will follow. This pattern establishment should be keenly observed when you wish to invest in a share.

The basic understanding is that, you have to look at the trend that the share has followed in the past and assume that it will follow the same trend in the future. Say for example that a stock has reached its highest at the beginning of the month and its lowest in the middle of a month. You must see if this has happened for more than two months and establish a pattern. Now, you will be wise to know when to buy and accumulate on the stocks and also when it is time to dispose them.

For this, you can study the graph of the shares. You will find that the price fluctuates and there is a certain pattern in the fluctuation. You can look at a one-year graph or a five-year graph. Once you understand it, you can invest in it accordingly.

Apart from looking at its graph, you must also look at its demand and supply volumes. Look at the volumes that are traded on a day-to-day basis. Is it too high or too low and are there enough buyers and sellers participating in its trade or not? These are some of the questions to ask when it comes to technical analysis of data.

There are many advantages to technical trading. The first one being establishing a set pattern with a stock! As you know, day trading requires you to buy and sell stocks within a short period of time. If you know how the stock will move, then you will make it easy on yourself. You will know the best time to buy them and the best time to sell. The second advantage is that, it will be faster for you to go through the graph and should not take you any more than 30 minutes to study the technical aspect of a stock.

However, there are certain disadvantages to using the technical technique as well. The first one being not considering anything apart from the stock's trend! If you don't consider the company's basics, then you will not know how the stocks will fare. Secondly, it is tough to predict whether or not a stock will tread the same path as it once did or whether it will take a different course. So over reliance on technical trading is not recommended.

Fundamentals

Apart from the technical aspects of a stock, you must also consider its fundamentals. Fundamental trading refers to considering the company's worth, while picking your stocks. As you know, all companies have a certain value and you must study it in detail to know where they stand. If you blindly pick stocks without understanding the company's true worth, then you might endanger your financial investments. Here are some things to consider while looking at a company's fundamentals.

Board members

Start by checking who the board members are. Also try and find out whether everybody on the board gets along fine or there are tiffs and internal bickering. If there are, then steer clear of such a company. If there aren't then the company is good to invest in. Ensure that you check its board election policy as well.

Dividends

Next check if they remain in profit and give away dividends. The amount of dividend a company gives away helps you determine whether it is a good company or not.

Balance sheet

Next up on the list is checking the balance sheet of the company. The balance sheet of the company will help you see how many assets they possess and how many liabilities they owe. If the assets are more than the liabilities then it is a good company but if the liabilities are more, then the company is not doing so well. Check how much debt they have and their debt repayment trend. If it is a big company capable of repaying its debts with ease, then you can pick their stocks.

Cash flow statement

The cash flow statement refers to looking at how much cash goes in and out of the company. You can see their working capital and assess whether they are doing well with their money management.

Income statement

The income statement refers to the income that the company is generating through its business. There will be both operating and non-operating incomes. Operating incomes are those that are generated through the company's main business. So if a company makes computers, its operating income is earned by selling these computers. Non-operating income refers to money received through other sources. Say for example that the company sells some of its assets and makes money - that money is non-operating income.

P/E ratio

The P/E ratio refers to the value of each share in the company, and you must look at their earnings per share. If the ratio is high then the company is good, but if the earnings are poor, then the company isn't doing that well.

There are many advantages to conducting a fundamental research, the first one being understanding whether the company is really good. You will know where it is headed and what makes it a good company. Remember to pick stocks of a big company that has a small market share as opposed to a small company with a big market share.

The disadvantage however is that, you will have to spend a lot of time studying the fundamentals of the company.

Contrarian trading

Contrarian trading refers to going against the grain while trading. The contrarian will choose to go the opposite direction to everybody . Contrarian trading is quite popular and you can consider it a good trading strategy for yourself.

When the price of a stock falls, most people will buy it but a contrarian will sell it. Similarly, when the prices of a stock are rising and everybody is selling their shares, the contrarian will buy it.

There are several advantages to this technique the main being getting more profit from your trade. You will know to predict the crowd's sentiment and invest accordingly.

The main disadvantage of this technique is that, the crowd might actually be selling their stocks after hearing some unfavorable news about the company. So it will be wise for you to dispose of your stocks as well.

James Carnegie

Chapter 12

Forecasting Methods

It is obvious that most of the strategies that are used to conduct day trading activities rely on "forecasting" as a means to predict what the market will look like. But how do these traders forecast? Well, let's find out.

Both experienced and inexperienced traders make use of forecasting techniques to arrive at decisive conclusions. These forecasting methods are

Patterns

The very first and most common method is using patterns. Patterns help the trader in forecasting the stock fluctuations. Through several years of research, experts have come up with some set patterns such as the triangle pattern, the evening star pattern, and the head and shoulders pattern, all of which aid in accurate predictions. This was stressed upon in the "candlestick" pattern strategy and is used to predict the rise and fall of stocks with accuracy.

Pivots

Pivots are used to understand the range of the price fluctuations. For the range pattern strategy, it is important to understand the entire range that the prices will use. This range consists of the highest rise on one side and the lowest fall on the other. Once the range is calculated using graph patterns and Fibonacci ratios, it will be easy to predict when the stocks will reach their high and when they will rapidly start to fall.

Fading

Fading refers to quickly selling stocks that are rising and is often used in contrarian strategy. As soon as the price of stocks starts to move upwards, the trader will dispose of them with the assumption that over-buying of the stocks will cause them to lose their value. It is evident that the contrarian view is opposed to the general view and therefore with fading, the trader will choose to sell when others will be looking to buy.

Average

When it comes to day trading, you will have to focus on three main points: the high, the low and the average. Remember that the average will always stay between the other two and you will have to understand where it lies in order to continue on a steady momentum. Once the average is established, the trader will know whether the prices are moving downwards or if they are moving upwards. He will know to slow down when the momentum is high and pick up speed when the momentum is slow.

Tells

This is for the news forecasts strategy. Here, the trader is looking at how the market is reacting to the news of a company declaring its profits or losses. Although it is extremely tough to interpret people's thoughts, it is possible to understand how a majority is thinking. So assume that Apple Inc. declared their profits and all the investors are extremely happy. The next day, you are sure to see a spike in the demand for Apple stocks. Now assume that they declare their next quarterly statement, and have not fared as well as the last time. The market might go into frenzy and the value of the stocks may drop the next day. So it helps to follow the news and understand how the market reacts to them in general.

Fundamentals

Another instrument that traders use to predict the stock value is fundamentals. Fundamentals basically refer to understanding the fundamentals of the company that the stocks belong to. Here, it is important to understand every small detail of the stock in order to predict the stock's value. Say for example that you are dealing in cotton as a commodity. If the cotton is grown in black soil, then it will thrive and you will have good quality cotton. But if it is grown in red, then it will be of poor quality. The price for both will differ tremendously and someone who is new to the business might overpay for a bunch of cotton grown in red soil. Therefore it is best to go into the minute details of the stock, the company, the commodity etc. before trading in it.

Sentiment

Sentiment technique refers to understanding the overall market mood. Although it is difficult to place the investors into specific groups, it is possible to predict how most of them are thinking. Once the trader is able to effectively predict the mood of the market, he or she will have the chance to make the right decisions. It is important to observe the market for a few days to understand the mood effectively. Don't be in a hurry to make your choice. Study the market first and then predict stock moves based on your observation.

Remember that all these techniques are used to speculate and will not give guarantee results. It is impossible to have guarantees in the stock market. Nothing is free from risk and these techniques are used to minimize them . You can make use of these to speculate on how the market will appear on a daily basis. At first, you might have a problem in understanding how it works but with time, and through regular practice, you will be able to predict well enough and increase your investment's potential.

James Carnegie

Chapter 13
Power Principles to Make Sure Your Trading Plan Work

Having a trading plan when investing in "options" is like having a roadmap when travelling to a new location; you already know where you are going, how long it takes, how much it costs you and other details a traveler must know to make the journey a success. No trader could ever survive the stock markets without a solid and implementable trading plan. So far in this book, you have learned:

• How to set your financial and trading goals.

• How to choose the right options market for your trading goals.

• The timeframe you should trade in.

• The different trading styles and how to pick the ideal style for you.

• Forecasting and day trading techniques that result in profitable trades.

When you have defined your goals and formulated your trading strategies, you need to see them through and ensure that they actually work. Having a solid plan is one thing, making it work is a totally different thing. Thus far, trading may seem great and you may feel confident about investing your money, but to make sure that the plans you have in place work, you need rules to govern how you start trading and how you conduct yourself before and during trades.

In this chapter of the eBook, I have put together ten essential principles to make your trading strategies a success. You should use these principles to scrutinize and evaluate your strategies, whether you developed them yourself or adopted them from a third party. You will dramatically increase your chances of success in day trading when you check your strategies against these important principles.

#1. Have Few Rules, It Makes It Easy to Understand and Follow Trading

You may find it surprising that the most effective trading systems often have less than ten rules. The more the rules a system has, the higher the chances that you will 'curve-fit' your strategy to past data. An over-optimized system is obviously very unlikely to make profits in real markets.

Besides being concise, it is important that the rules that guide your trading strategy are easy to understand and execute. Day trading markets are known to behave wildly and to move very fast and in most cases you will not even have the time to make long calculations with complicated formulas to make important trading decisions. Successful floor traders arm themselves with a pen and a paper, or just an electronic calculator to do simple calculations but they make thousands of dollars every day.

#2. Trade Liquid and Electronic Markets

Options trades are fast paced, and as such, it is highly recommended that you stick to electronic markets. This is not only because their commissions are much lower but also because you will receive fills instantly. You will want to know as soon as your order is filled and at what price since your exit plan is based on this information. You must never set an exit order before you know what the entry order is.

When you trade in liquid markets, you cannot afford any slippages, which can cost you tens, hundreds even thousands of dollars. With open outcry markets (non-electronic markets), you may be forced to wait a few seconds or minutes before you receive your fill. By this time, market conditions may already have turned and a potentially profitable trade could have turned into a loss. Fortunately, more and more markets today have switched to electronic trading. This is just a good piece of advice in case you have your eyes on markets that still conduct trades in an "old school" manner.

#3: Set Realistic Expectations

At the beginning of this book, you learned that day trading presents an opportunity to make huge profits from stocks as well as the potential to make serious losses. There is no trading system that has no losses. If you ever come across a system that promises 100% profitability, it is too good to be true and sadly, just isn't true. A robust options trading system can have:

- A win percentage of between 50 and 80 percent.

- A profit factor of between 1.25 and 2.5.

- A maximum drawdown of 10 to 20 percent of the annual profit.

These numbers are a rough guideline that you can use to easily identify a curve-fitted system that promises instant riches with no risks. As discussed in Chapter 11 of this book, there are various risks you have to bear in mind even before you make a firm decision to invest your money in day trading.

#4. Strike A Healthy Balance Between Risk and Reward

The unpredictable nature of day trading means that there is always a chance of making a profit or a loss. If you walk into a casino for instance, and bet all your money on 'red' in a game of roulette, you will have a 49 percent chance of doubling your money as well as a 51 percent chance of losing everything. Likewise, with stock trading, you can make a lot of money when you risk a lot, but the risk is very high. It is imperative that you find a balance between the risks you are willing to take and the rewards you want to realize.

Ensure that you have a workable trading strategy that has small stop losses and that the profit targets are greater than your stop losses. You must never use a strategy that has a small profit margin of say $100 and a stop loss of $1,000. The winning percentage is fantastic, that's true, but if you suffer 1 or 2 losses in a row, they will completely wipe out your trading account.

A reasonable balance between risk and reward should be something like 1:1.5. This means that for every $1 you risk, you should be able to make at least $1.50. Plainly put, if you set a stop loss of $100, you should have a profit target of at least $150.

#5. Select Systems Producing at Least Five Trades Per Week

The higher the number of trades you execute, the lower the chances of you have of making losses in a month. If your trading strategy presents a 70 percent winning potential, but you only execute one trade in a month, one loss would be enough to render your entire monthly venture a loss. Considering that it is possible to suffer several consecutive losing trades, unless your choice of trades presents a higher trading frequency, you risk losing hundreds and even thousands of dollars in bad trades before you realize a single profit.

It is best to have a marketing strategy that produces at least five trades in a single week so that you can have at least 20 trades in a month. In such cases, a winning percentage of 70 tremendously increases the chances of executing profitable trades in a single month. In the end, just like every other trader, your objective would be to have as many profitable months as possible.

#6. Start Small and Grow Big Gradually

There are many reasons why it is recommended that you make small investments at the beginning of your day trading practice. Top among these reasons are the risks associated with such an investment and the importance of getting familiar with how the market works before making huge financial commitments. While developing or selecting a workable trading strategy, it is best to find one that allows you to start with small trades and increase gradually.

A great trading system would ideally allow you to begin with one or two contracts and depending on the outcomes, increase or maintain the position as your trading account grows.

You must never use the *'martingale'* trading strategy unless you are certain of what you are doing. This is a trading strategy that requires you to double your investment every time you lose with a promise that at some point down the line, you will win back all the money you lost in previous trades.

#7. Test Your Strategy On at Least 200 Trades

How can you be sure that your trading strategy will work? The best approach is to thoroughly test it using back testing without curve fitting, to increase the probability of it succeeding in future trades.

Number of trades	50	100	200	300	400	500

Margin of Error	17%	15%	12%	10%	7%	5%

The higher the number of trades executed in back-testing mode, the smaller the margin of error, hence the higher the probability of producing profitable trades in the future. In order to perform a valid performance report, you need to execute at least 40 trades. From the above example, the optimal number of trades is 300 with an error margin of just 10%.

The important principles to follow should enable you to track your progress and help you realize a healthy trading approach with a greater percentage of winning trades compared to losing trades. There is no doubt that any strategy that has smaller winning percentages can be profitable, but the important element in this point is the psychological effect of pressure, which can be enormous and can cause traders to make mistakes. As a beginner, it is imperative that you adopt a strategy that will not only result in profitable trades but will also boost your confidence in trading, preferably with winning margins of over 60% to start with.

James Carnegie

Chapter 14

Penny Stocks

Penny stocks refer to those stocks that are valued less than $5. These stocks are quite cheap and are accessible to everyone. The reason why these stocks are preferred is because of the changes that occur on their price on a daily basis. There will be a radical difference in their price and by the time you sell them, you will have made a lot of profit.

Penny stocks are not always traded in the stock market and are bought and sold over the counter. You have to familiarize yourself with paper trading. Paper trading refers to making use of papers to denote money, as you will not be required to pull out your money while trading in these stocks.

These shares mostly belong to those companies that have a low market capture but that should not deter you from investing in them, as you are not really concerned about their progress and only interested in the changes of their share prices.

The basic idea is to buy a large volume of these stocks when they reach their daily lowest price and then quickly sell them when they reach their highest. You will walk away with a handsome profit by doing so, but you have to study the stock for a while to know how it will behave. Don't assume all penny stocks will help you as only a few will fare well on a daily basis. You have to identify these and trade with them.

Advantages of penny stocks

There are many advantages of trading in penny stocks. The first advantage being, their low prices! So there is no need for you to invest a lot of money into it. You can start low and still avail of many stocks.

The second advantage is that the stocks will move up in no time at all. You don't have to wait for a long time for the prices to move up. They will generally shoot up within a couple of hours. If you are holding the stock when dividends are being announced, then you will be able to profit from it in two ways.

Once you start trading in penny stocks, you will not feel like trading in your regular stocks because it will be that lucrative.

Disadvantages of penny stocks

There are certain disadvantages attached with this type of stocks. The main disadvantage is that, there might not be enough information about these stocks available for people to invest in them. People might not be aware that such stocks exist and they might not trade with them. Many brokers will refuse to help you as they will not be aware of the stocks and wonder if you will pin blame on them for having picked the wrong stocks.

Another disadvantage is the volumes traded. Penny stocks will not have large volumes when being traded. There will just be a few stocks that are bought and sold and so, the movement in price might be low. So you have to pick stocks that have large trading volumes. You might not have the chance to liquidate your penny stocks, which can cause you to take a loss on them.

If a pump and dump scam is rampant, then you might become a victim. These are scams where a group of people will force a lot of people to buy shares of a company and increase its per share value. These people will then quickly sell their share. This will cause the shares value to plummet. You might end up buying when the prices are high and not be able to sell them when they plummet or sell them at a loss.

Chapter 15

Risks to Consider and Avoid

When it comes to day trading, there are certain things you must bear in mind in order to minimize the risks. Some of these tips are as follows

Financial Risks

These are the very first things that you need to consider when you decide to start day trading. Here are some things to bear in mind before you start.

Don't Invest Too Much

Remember to not gamble with a lot of your money. The day trading market is quite volatile and the trend is difficult to predict. You might not have the same kind of prices prevailing through the day and might end up with a loss at the end. For this purpose, you have to be cautious with how much money you invest into it. As a rule of thumb, one should invest the same amount on a daily basis and not increase the amount he puts into stocks. Remember that you will have several opportunities to increase the value of your money and there is no need to rush into it with large amounts. Decide on a sum and make sure that you invest only that much on a daily basis. After a month or two, you can increase the amount slightly and then maintain the same for another month or two and so on and so forth. You must familiarize yourself with the concept of risk capital. Risk capital refers to whatever money you are willing to lose in the stock market. When you have calculated your risk, you can trade confidently. Say for example, you think you will lose $1,000 in the market. You have calculated your risk here. But for that risk, you must also calculate the profit you will receive if things go well in the market. Let's say for example, $2,000. So even if you do lose the $1,000, you still walk away with a profit of $1,000. And if things go your way then you walk away with the $2000. So you must calculate your risk at the very beginning.

Don't Expect Too Much

It is wise not to expect too much gain out of your investment. That means, do not expect to make huge profits within a short period of time. You will not have the chance to become a millionaire overnight just because you have started day trading. The markets can be volatile and will not allow you to break into a huge profit overnight. If you expect too much then you will be disappointed. So try not to expect too much from your investments and have reasonable expectations. It might take a few months or even a couple of years before you start to make a steady profit. Until then, you must remain persistent and do everything that is beneficial for your investment business. Remember that the initial amount you put in matters quite a bit and your profit will be based on how much you invest. So by investing $200 you can look at a profit of, let's say $50, and not $2,000. Your profits will ultimately be cumulative.

Beware of Losses

Remember to always factor in your losses. No investment is free from losses and you will have to consider them when you wish to start day trading. Everybody knows that the share market is extremely volatile and one that is hard to pin down. If you remain ignorant of your losses, then you might be in big trouble. Look at your monthly graphs and calculate the number of times you have suffered a loss. Once you have the numbers, try and work on your investment plans to reduce your losses. But beware; there will be no eradicating your losses, as a constant winning streak is never a reality. You have to remain wary of stocks and securities that you think will cause you losses and try and avoid investing in them as much as you can, in order to substantially cut down on the losses.

Career Risks

When it comes to day trading, here are some career risks that you might face.

Not the Main Career

Remember that you cannot consider day trading as your main job, especially if you are just starting out. Do not hastily quit your day job just because you have scored a day trading gig. You must hold on to your job until you are well established as a day trader. It is hard to predict how long this might take but a couple of years is a good estimation. Even if you are making a good profit as soon as you start trading, you must wait it out to see if you can continue making similar profits. Once you garner the confidence, you can choose to become a full time day trader. But remember, do not think you will start to make just as much as your day job pays you within a couple of months of going full time with it. It might take a little more time but eventually it will be possible for you to match and even surpass your salary.

Parallel Income

Day trading is a great source of parallel income. Along with your active income, you will have a chance to have a portfolio income as well. For this, you will have to take it seriously though. There can be those who will take it casually and invest in day trading as a pastime. Doing so, however, will cost you and you might have to suffer losses. So don't take day trading casually and look at it as a good alternate source of income. You can decide to spend the money that you make through day trading in paying your bills and save more in a month. Whatever is left is what is used to fuel your day trading investments. As was mentioned earlier, you must treat day trading as a parallel source of income and hold on to your day job in order to establish financial stability.

Productivity

One aspect that worries most day traders is the number of hours they have to spend staring at a computer screen to look at the trends. This will cause them to waste quite a bit of time doing nothing and as a result, might cause them to miss out on several good opportunities. Therefore, it is advisable to indulge in day trading in your spare time, as you will have free time on your hands. If you are keen on day trading while at work, then you can consider hiring a discounted broker and keep an eye on the trends. As soon as you see an opportunity, you can call him up and buy or sell the stock. If you have the resources for it,you can consider hiring a full service broker for the weekdays and indulge in day tradingpersonally, on the weekends.

Social Life

Just like how people worry about not being productive while indulging in day trading, there is also the fear of losing out on a social life. For this, it is best to indulge in day trading whenever time permits and not compromise your social life. It is possible for you to trade on any day that you like and take a couple of days off to socialize. Similarly, don't put your life on the back burner -pamper yourself from time to time. You need not take day trading extremely seriously and must try and enjoy life to the fullest. Maybe even consider taking a vacation just to chill out and not think of day trading.

Health Risks

Just like career and financial risks, there are some health risks that you must be aware of that day trading can cause. They are as follows

Mental Strength

Day trading can take a lot of thinking and cause you to drain away mentally. For this, you must try and remain as mentally strong as possible. You can indulge in solving mind games and make sure that you are not feeling lazy or fatigued. Have a puzzle book handy and try and solve some puzzles in order to remain alert. You can consider playing a game on the computer such as chess in order strengthen your mental ability. If it is getting too overwhelming, then consider taking a break and taking a walk outside. You can also play with your children or pets and reduce some of the pressure on your mind. Do whatever works best for you and aim to maintain a calm state of mind.

Emotional Support

During the initial phase, you will have a lot of enthusiasm and will begin day trading with quite a bit of fervor. But as time passes, you will realize that the activities are perhaps draining you emotionally and that you are feeling tired. You will have to take care of your finances, you will need to consider your family's needs etc. and all of it might start to feel overwhelming. For this, you need to have emotional support from friends and family members who will stand by you, regardless of whether you are suffering a loss or making a profit. Just remember that you have to go through it and not give up on it half way through.

Health Issues

There are some other health issues that day trading can cause such as hypertension, high blood pressure and also hyperventilation. For all these, it is best that you indulge in things that make you happy so that you can keep these ill effects at bay. If you suffer from high blood pressure already, then have a self-monitoring kit handy in order to check yourself from time to time. As was said earlier, do not take up day trading so seriously that it starts to take over your life. Try and remain calm and composed and you will realize that you are trading better. Have in mind that day trading is meant to be a parallel source of income and a long-term investment that will help you secure your future.

Remember that these are mere precautionary measures that are mentioned so that you can avoid negative symptoms and are not meant to discourage you from taking up day trading. Day trading is a great option for both new and old investors and will help you in diversifying your investment options.

James Carnegie

Chapter 16
Common Mistakes New Option Traders Make

This chapter of the eBook analyzes ten of the most common mistakes that newcomers in option trading often make. By nature, "options" are a more complex form of stocks investment compared to outright buying and selling company stocks. For instance, to profitably trade in "options", you must know which direction the stock prices are heading and you must be right about the timing of purchase and sale point. Also, compared to stocks, "options" tend to be less liquid and trading in them involve greater spreads between the bid and the ask prices. If you just fell off the turnip truck, "options" are not something you want to dive fully into.

Mistake 1: Buying Out-Of-The-Money (OTM) Call Options While Starting Out

I wouldn't blame you for thinking that this is the perfect place to start: buying a call "option" then waiting to see if you can pick a winner. If you have traded in equity before, buying calls may feel like a safe trading strategy because it matches the pattern you have traded in before: simply buy low and sell high. After all, many veteran equity traders learned to trade and excelled in profiting from such investment the same way.

The reason why buying out-of-the-money calls outright, is not the best starting strategy is because it is one of the hardest ways to make money consistently in "options" trading. Limiting yourself to this single strategy can certainly lead you to consistently losing money and not learning very much on how to trade or make a decent profit. When starting out in "options" trading, consider getting a crash course in several other trading strategies to improve your earning potential and build your knowledge. Learning a few trading strategies online or from "options" trading books increases your potential of earning a solid profit and reduces your chances of losing money.

Why Not Just Buy Calls?

Calling the direction on stock before purchase is tough enough. With "options" though, you must be certain about which direction the stock is heading and you must time the purchase and sale points properly. If you get either of these essential elements wrong, your trade may result in the loss of the option premium you paid.

Each day that passes when the underlying stock does not move, your "option" is like an ice cube sitting in the sun. The time value of your "options" evaporates until the expiration date. This is especially true when your first purchase happens to be a near-term, way out-of-the-money "option", a popular method with newbie "options" traders for the reason that they are often very cheap.

There is a reason that out-of-the-money call "options" are cheap. When you purchase one, it does not increase automatically just because the stock moves in the right direction. Its price is relative to the probability of the stock reaching or exceeding the strike price. This means that the probability of the stock continuing to move in the shortening timeframe is low if the move is close to expiration, and it is not enough to reach the strike. Therefore, the "option" price is essentially a reflection of that probability.

How Can You Be More Informed as A Newbie?

When you first venture into "options" trading, you should consider first selling an out-of-the-money call on stock that you already own in a strategy commonly called 'covered call'. When you sell the call, you will be taking the obligation to sell the stock at the strike price listed in the "option". This means that if the strike price is higher than the current market price of the stock, you will be "okaying" the buyer to 'call' or buy the stock away from you when the stock exceeds the strike price. This is the surest way to earn cash from the sale of your out-of-the-money call. The strategy works on the principle that you earn income on stocks when you are bullish and you wouldn't mind selling the stock when the price goes up before expiration.

Mistake 2: Adopting an "All-Purpose" Strategy in Every Market Condition

As I mentioned in chapter 1, "options" trading is a remarkably flexible form of stocks investment. It allows you to trade effectively in almost all kinds of market conditions and still make insane profits. However, you can only take advantage of such flexibility when you stay open to learning and applying new strategies.

A great way to capitalize on different market conditions is by buying spreads, also known as 'long spreads'. If you are a new "options" trader, it is highly recommended that you familiarize yourself with the possibilities and opportunities of spreads, so you can start to recognize the right conditions of using them and generate profits.

What Exactly Are Long Spreads and How Beneficial Are They?

Simply put, a long spread is a position consisting of two options: a higher cost and a lower cost set of "options". The higher cost "option" position is the buying position while the lower cost "option" is the selling position. These are very similar "options", featuring the same underlying security, the same number of contracts, the same expiration dates and the same types of positions (both are either calls or puts). The only difference between them is their strike price. A long spread made up of calls is a "bullish" position and is known as a 'long call spread' while a long spread made up of puts bears a "bearish" position and is referred to as a 'long put spread'.

When you buy one spread trade "option" at the same time that you sell another, the time decay that could have hurt one leg may actually help the other. This means that when you trade spreads, the net effect of time decay is neutralized compared to buying individual "options".

There is however a downside to trading spreads. Your upside potential is limited by the counter calls or puts. Frankly, very few call buyers ever make sky-high profits when they engage in spread trades because most of the time, when the stocks hit a certain price, they will sell it anyway. So, why not just set the sell target when entering the trade. It is however important to mention that, even though long spreads limit the maximum gain potential, they also limit the maximum loss potential.

There are two downsides to consider before engaging in spread trading. Firstly, because this strategy involves multiple "option" trades, it incurs multiple commissions. Ensure that your profit and loss calculations cater for the commissions along with other factors such as bid and ask spreads. Secondly, as with every other new strategy, you must first understand the risks before committing any capital to long call spreads or long put spreads.

Mistake 3: Failing to Set Definite Exit Plans Preceding Expiration

You have heard it a thousand times before; just like stocks, with "options" trading, it is critical that you do not let your emotions interfere with your trades. This does not mean that you swallow your every fear and turn into a stone; it simply means that you make a plan to work on, and follow that plan. A very important part of this plan is having an exit point where you can minimize your losses in the event of a downslide.

Even when things are going your way, you must always have an exit plan. Seasoned day traders advise that you set your downside exit point in advance of your upside exit point while you set the timeframes for your trades.

What if you set exit points and get out too early, won't that leave some upside on the table?

The classic trader's worry is losing out on a great profit because the exit point is too close. The best counterargument I can come up with is: what if you consistently make a good profit, reduce the chances of making losses and get to sleep better at night? When you plan ahead and get used to setting exit points, you establish better trading patterns and get to keep your worries in check while trading "options".

Why Are Exit Points Important?

Whether you are selling or buying "options", having an exit plan is mandatory. Decide in advance what gains you will be contented with on the upside and decide the worst-case scenario that you can afford in case of a downside. When your trade reaches the upside goal you set, clear the position and take your profits. Most new "options" trades lose out because they get greedy. When your trade reaches the downside stop-loss point, once again, clear your position and accept the loss. Do not make the mistake of exposing yourself to great risks by gambling on price "options" bouncing right back.

From time to time, you will have a strong temptation to violate this advice when your position is spiraling down fast. This is where you absolutely have to lock your emotions out of your trades and stick to the plan.

Mistake 4: Trading in Illiquid Options

Liquidity in trading is how fast a trader can purchase or sell something without causing a substantial price movement. A liquid market constantly has readily active buyers and sellers throughout the trading period. A more elegant, mathematical way to see a liquid market is the probability that a trade will be executed at a price equal to the previous one.

Compared to "options", stock markets are more "liquid" for the simple reason that traders are often buying and selling just one stock, unlike "option" traders who may be trading in dozens of contracts at a particular time. Because of this, stock traders will often flock to purchase and sell one form of stock e.g. Apple stocks, but "options" traders may have five different expirations of the same stock and a ton of strike prices to choose from. By definition, "options'" trading presents more choices and as such, the market will not be as liquid as the traditional stock market.

Of course, Apple will not present a liquidity problem for "options" or stock traders because its stocks are being constantly traded. The problem comes in with smaller stocks, e.g. HyperGreenTech, an imaginary environmentally friendly energy startup showing some promise, but whose stocks are traded once a week and by appointment only. If this company's stock is illiquid, its "options" are most likely to be inactive. This would cause an artificially wide spread between the bid and the ask "options" price. It is never a good idea to trade in illiquid "options" with wide bid-ask spreads.

Why Shouldn't You Trade in Illiquid Options?

Trading in illiquid "options" drives up the cost of doing business and with the already high percentage costs of "options" trading; it would be an unnecessary burden on the trader.

In this case, the rule of thumb to follow is: when you trade in "options", ensure that the open interest is equal to at least 40 times the number of contacts you intend to trade. You can save yourself added stress and costs of "options" trading by choosing to trade in liquid opportunities only.

Mistake 5: Waiting too Long to Buy Your Short Options Back

Far too often, new "option" traders wait for too long before they buy back the "options" they have sold. There are many reasons why they do this: they don't want to pay the commission; they are betting the contract will expire with no value; or hoping to squeeze out a little more profit from the trade.

This mistake boils down to just one piece of advice: you must always be willing and ready to buy back short "options" early. Don't be cheap. If a short "option" goes way out-of-the-money and you are in a position to buy it back and the purchase would take the risk off the table profitably, go ahead and do it.

For example, if you sold an "option" worth $1.00 and now it is worth $0.20, you obviously wouldn't sell the 20-cent "option", because it wouldn't be worth it. Similarly, you shouldn't assume that there is value in squeezing the last few cents out of such a trade.

Mistake 6: Failing to Factor in Dividend or Earnings Payment Dates into Your Options Strategy

It is important that you keep track of the dividend and earning dates for your underlying stock when trading "options". For instance, if you sell calls and there is a dividend approaching, the probability that you may be assigned early increases. This is particularly true if the expected dividend is large because "option" owners do not have rights to dividends. In order to collect dividends, "option" traders have to exercise the option and actually buy the underlying stock.

Early assignments are random, hard-to-control threats for "options" traders. However, impending dividends is one of the few elements that you can identify and even control to reduce the possibility of being assigned.

The earning season often makes "options" contracts pricier, for both calls and puts. During this time, it is important to think in real-world terms: that "options" work like protection contracts that can hedge the risk on other positions. For instance, a trader living in Florida would realize that a homeowner's insurance would be most expensive when the weatherman predicts a home-wrecking hurricane. This principle can be used to determine "options" trades during the earnings seasons. Pending news of earnings can trigger volatility in the prices of stocks, and as such, a trader must be aware of doing business during such a season.

It is fine if you wish to trade stocks specifically during the earnings season. Just be aware of the increased volatility that will most likely also increase "option" premiums. For a beginner, it is best to steer clear of "options" during this season and venture back to trading after the effects of an earnings announcement have been absorbed into the market. Also, unless you are willing to accept higher risks of announcement, it is best to steer clear of "option" contracts with pending dividends. One alternative to consider if you have to buy an "option" during the earnings season is to buy one and sell another, thereby creating a spread.

Mistake 7: Failing to Factor in The Possibility of Being Assigned

Early assignment is one of those very emotional, usually irrational market events that can happen for no particular reason. Sometimes, it just happens even when it is clear that it is not the most brilliant manoeuver at the time. The best defense against early assignment is to factor it into your trading plans early. Otherwise, it may force you to execute defensive in-the-moment trading decisions that are unlikely to be logical when they happen.

When you exercise a call, it means that you are a trader willing to spend cash to buy a particular underlying stock now and not later in the game. It is an understandable facet of human nature to want to wait and spend money later. However, in the event of stock rising, it is not uncommon for less skilled traders to pull the trigger early, thereby failing to realize that they are leaving some premium on the trading table. This is the reason why early assignment can be so unpredictable.

General tips

As you know, the stock market is full of ups and down and you must tread carefully if you wish to remain in profit. Here are some general tips for you to ponder over when you wish to enter the stock market.

Flexibility

Try to remain flexible with your investment options. Don't make up your mind on just one type of stock and keep your options open. If you decide to buy a certain stock in the morning but get a call to choose another one, then pick the better of the two instead of being too rigid with it. You must also be flexible in terms of the markets that you choose to invest in. If it's a "bullish" market and a particular stock is doing badly, dispose of it instead of waiting on it to rise in value. The opposite applies to a "bearish" market.

Control

Learn to perform controlled trading. Don't try to explore all the options that the market puts forth and remain in your limits. If a stock is good, then don't over buy. As was mentioned earlier, you should invest no more than 5% in any one stock and try to plan it in such a way that you have 5% in several different securities. If your broker keeps calling you to suggest shares, then ask him to take it slowly and not pressure you.

Make up your mind

It is extremely important that you exit from your position at the end of the day when you wish to day trade. It will be very tempting for you to stay put and hold on to stocks of a company to capitalize on any overnight points gained. But you will not know when to exit and end up holding on to stocks that you should have disposed of a long time back. Therefore, try to not get emotionally attached with a stock and dispose of it to book profits.

Real not paper

Remember that your real profits are always better than your paper profits. If you don't capitalize on them and transfer the profits into your account, then you will be making a big mistake. Don't keep checking your account without capitalizing on it. You never know when the markets will start behaving badly and it is better to book profits when you have the chance to.

Diversify

Diversify your investments as much as possible. Don't invest in the same stocks over and over again. Diversify it in such a way that all your risk is spread. Pick a few stocks, some commodities, invest in mutual funds etc. This will ensure that you remain in profit and the loss from one type of investment is countered by the profit from another investment.

Confidence

Remember to go with your gut feeling when you wish to trade in the stock market. Have the confidence to take risks and benefit from them. If you have chosen a strategy for yourself then be assured that you will make money out of it and don't doubt yourself.

Learn daily

Take away a lesson on a daily basis and maintain a record of it somewhere. You must then refer back to it and understand what you did and where. You must also know to identify a situation and implement a plan of action based on your previous incidents. Don't be too rigid and promise yourself that you will take a new experience with you every single day.

Company

Remain in the company of avid traders. It will ensure that you take all the right steps and invest in all the best stocks. Consult with them from time to time and pick stocks that they are investing in. It is always better to go with an expert's opinion and buy stocks of companies that they have studied. They will get it right most of the times and you can benefit from it.

Patience

Patience is a virtue in the stock market. Ensure that you remain as patient as possible, especially, during the early stages. Once everything is set up, you can begin day trading. If you hurry into something, then it will not work well for you.

Key Takeaways

"Options" trading refer to choosing "options" that you can either buy in full or refuse to buy. The option lies with you. If you think you will get a good deal out of it then go ahead with it but if you think it is not working to your advantage, then dispose it. "Options" can have any underlying financial security ranging from stocks to commodities to foreign currencies. You must choose the one that will give you the best benefits.

There are many advantages of "options" and you must go through each of them to evaluate their true benefit. "Options" are a good choice, as they will allow you to hedge and safeguard your investments. However, there are also several disadvantages of "options" that you must familiarize yourself with if you wish to capitalize on your investment. Remember that "options" are traded in the stock market and you must gain some knowledge on that before you start trading.

Stock markets refer to those markets where shares are bought and sold on a daily basis. These markets can be physical or virtual. Physical markets are those where brokers converge on the floor of the market to buy and sell stocks whereas virtual markets are those where people buy and sell stocks without being physically present in the market. You can choose either, depending on your investment needs.

To get started, you must first open an account in a brokerage firm and then create an account. You must then transfer your trading money into this account. You will receive a login ID and password that you can use to log into your account. You can then choose a broker to work with. Try to pick a good one and it is a good idea to pick a full time broker if you wish to capitalize on your investment.

Create an office at home for yourself by setting up a computer and a reliable internet connection. These are extremely important if you wish to trade on a daily basis. You will have to make quick decisions and buy and sell at the drop of a hat. If you have a slow connection, then you might end up losing out on a lucrative deal. So ensure that there are no issues when you trade in the stock market and everything works smoothly.

Stocks are shares of a company that are traded in the market on a daily basis. You have to pick stocks of those companies that are doing well. Since you will be carrying out day trading, you will buy and sell on a daily basis and so, must have a pre determined trading amount to begin with. But it is best to start small and then increase the value as you go. Starting out big might cause you to spend more than you can afford.

Commodities are also traded in the share market on a daily basis. These include metals, livestock, agricultural produce, chemicals etc. All of these are valued at a certain price and then sold at a different price to ring in a profit.

Just like commodities, precious metals and foreign currencies are also traded in the stock market. You can buy and sell these as you please, on a day-to-day basis. The basic motive is to buy them at a low price and then sell them at a high price.

You have to make use of prediction techniques to predict the prices of the stocks. There are a few methods to use such as news forecasts and trend analysis, which will give you a fair idea of the stocks to pick. Go through them again to know why each one is different from the other and how you can use them to your advantage.

You can trade in penny stocks if you like. These stocks are low priced and you can buy them in large volumes. The main intention of trading in these is to capitalize on their price differences. You must know how to pick the best penny stocks and deal in them to realize a profit. But there are certain disadvantages attached with them and you must familiarize yourself with them before you start trading.

There are also certain trading methods such as the contrarian method, the fundamental and technical analysis. You must understand what each of these signifies and then use them to analyze the stocks. You have to pick them based on your findings. You must spend some time in understanding the stocks and not jump into it without doing due research.

There are two types of market conditions known as the "bullish" and "bearish" markets. You have to understand what both of these imply and know how to invest in them. You should also understand how they might reverse and what you must do in such a situation.

There are some health and career risks that trading in the stock market can put forth and you need to be aware of them to fully understand what you are getting yourself into.

There are several mistakes to avoid when it comes to day trading and we looked at them in detail. It is best that you go through them again just to be aware of the pitfalls in the share market and how you can avoid them.

Remember to be wise and diligent and try not to make too many mistakes when you trade in the stock market. Try to do your own research, and not jump into the trading process without calculating your risk. A little hard work, at the very beginning, will go a long way in helping you remain in profit.

Conclusion

Thank you for reading this book, I hope you not only had fun reading it but also got a lot of information about "options" trading that you found useful.

It is essential to know that "options" trading is very lucrative only if done the right way. It carries loads of risks that can be managed only if studied correctly. "Options" provide loads of opportunities for a normal person to make money. It is not rocket science to understand it.

The higher the risk, the higher the return is on the investment but for someone who wants to play it safe, it also has enough security cover to safeguard his/her investment.

I hope you have understood everything that it takes to start making day trading a reality for you and benefit from its high pay offs.

Please go ahead and increase your investment portfolio but ensure precaution while doing so.

Happy Investing.

www.ingramcontent.com/pod-product-compliance
Lightning Source LLC
Chambersburg PA
CBHW051905170526
45168CB00001B/255